Return to Terror Cove

10

Return to Terror Cove

Paul Buchanan
Created by Paul Buchanan and Rod Randall

BROADMAN
& HOLMAN
PUBLISHERS
Nashville, Tennessee

0–8054–2333–8

Published by Broadman & Holman Publishers,
Nashville, Tennessee

Dewey Decimal Classification: Fiction
Subject Heading: CHRISTIAN LIFE—JUVENILE FICTION
Library of Congress Card Catalog Number: 00-058610

All Scripture quotations are from The Holy Bible, New
International Version (NIV) © 1973, 1978, 1984 International Bible
Society; used by permission.

Library of Congress Cataloging-in-Publication Data
Buchanan, Paul, 1959–
    Return to Terror Cove / Paul Buchanan ; created by Paul
Buchanan and Rod Randall.
        p. cm.—(Heebie Jeebies series ; v. 10)
    Summary: After seeing a bad horror movie filmed years
ago in the coastal town where his father is the lighthouse
keeper, thirteen-year-old Danny suspects that a sea monster has returned in real life to recreate the events of the
film.
    ISBN 0–8054–2333–8 (pb)
        [1. Sea monsters—Fiction. 2. Lighthouses—Fiction.
    3. Christian life—Fiction. 4. Horror stories.] I. Randall,
Rod, 1962– II. Title. III. Series.
    PZ7.B87717 Re 2001
    [Fic]—dc21   00-058610
                                                              CIP

1 2 3 4 5   05 04 03 02 01

DEDICATION

For Danny,
who really lives on Lighthouse Point,
and his good friend, Josh.

Other books in the Heebie Jeebies series

Chapter 1

My name's Danny. I'm named after the guy in the Bible—Daniel, the one who got thrown in the den of lions—and I live out on Lighthouse Point with my mom and dad and kid sister. When I tell people I live in a lighthouse, they usually fall all over themselves cooing about how wonderful that must be and how lucky I am. But let me tell you: it's no picnic.

Most lighthouses are about a hundred years old, and they tend to be isolated. The rooms are small and cold. The phone goes out practically every time there's a storm. There's only one electrical outlet in each room. And try sleeping at night with a bright light passing by your bedroom window every thirty seconds and a big old foghorn blaring away in your backyard.

And that's just the beginning. Imagine how annoying it would be if every tourist who drove by came tramping through your front yard to get a picture of your house because it was so "quaint" and "picturesque." And when they're done taking pictures, they all want to ask you questions, as if you're some kind of tour guide. Sometimes they want to take pictures with *you,* like you're one of those costumed characters at a theme park. *Smile, Junior. Put your arm around him. OK, that's great. Now let's get another one with the whole family.*

Sure it's cool to be so near the ocean—but we're not near anything else. We're way out on Lighthouse Point to the north of Boulder Bay. It's a mile up the highway and a twenty-minute walk into town if the weather's really good—which it hardly ever is. We get a lot of rain up here, and when we don't have rain, we have fog. Did I mention the foghorn?

I shouldn't complain so much. I actually like it out here. It's beautiful. I like watching the ocean. Ships pass by Lighthouse Point all the time, along with migrating whales and big pods of dolphins. And I love boating. I have my own little skiff that I can take across the bay into town when the water isn't too choppy.

Life in a lighthouse is no picnic, but it suits me. I wouldn't move inland for all the fish in the sea.

Anyway, it was June, and school had just let out, so I was feeling free and full of high expectations. The sky above the lighthouse was slate gray that afternoon, and so was the ocean. It didn't look at all the way summer was supposed to, but the gloomiest day of summer vacation seems sunnier than a clear sky in April when you're taking a math test.

I was downstairs at the kitchen counter, making myself a turkey sandwich for lunch and trying to fend off my little sister, Bonnie the Vegetarian.

"You should feel terrible," she told me, hovering at my elbow as I piled cold cuts on a slice of bread. "That turkey was once a living, breathing creature."

I looked down at the sandwich. "You're right," I said. "But it's probably too late to save it now."

Bonnie crossed her arms and glared at me with one eyebrow raised.

What did she want from me? I bent over the sandwich and pretended to do CPR. After a few seconds I stopped and put my ear close to the cold cuts, listening for breathing. I looked at Bonnie and shook my head. "We did everything we could," I told her gravely. "But we just couldn't save him."

Bonnie glared at me again, not in the least bit amused.

I spread on a little mayonnaise and put the other slice of bread on top. "I guess there's nothing to do now but dispose of the remains," I said. I picked up the plate and carried it to the kitchen table, Bonnie at my heels.

"You're a barbarian," she informed me. "How would you like it if a giant monster wanted to eat *you* for lunch? What would you say then?"

I thought about it a few seconds. What *would* I say in such a situation? *"Aaaaaaaaaaaa,"* I suddenly screamed at the top of my lungs.

Bonnie jumped. Her eyes grew wide. "What's wrong?" she pleaded. "What happened?"

"Nothing," I told her. "I'm just answering your question. That's what I'd probably say if a monster was going to eat me." I took a bite of the sandwich.

"You think you're hilarious, don't you?" Bonnie said as I chewed.

I swallowed. "I have my moments."

Bonnie crossed her arms again. "Well, I hope it *does* happen some day," she told me. "Being eaten by a monster is nothing less than you deserve. And believe me, Danny—when it happens, I'll be standing by with a jar of mayo."

The phone rang. Bonnie ignored it.

"Aren't you going to answer that?" I asked her. "I'm busy eating a turkey sandwich, in case you haven't noticed."

"You can get it yourself," Bonnie said. "It's probably for you anyway." She turned, walked right by the ringing phone on the counter and out the kitchen door.

I shook my head and pushed back my chair. *Sisters!* I went over and picked up the phone.

"Hey, Danny," the voice on the other end said. "Sail that little boat of yours into town today. There's something you've got to see. You won't believe it." It was Josh. He's my best friend. We go to the same school *and* the same church, so I know him pretty well. He lives across the cove in Boulder Bay. I hadn't seen him in the week since school let out.

"It's not a little boat; it's a skiff," I told him. Josh lived in an inn a block from the ocean, but he knew nothing about sailing. "And since when do you have time to hang out during tourist season? I thought you had to help run the inn."

Josh lowered his voice, as if he didn't want his mom to overhear. "Are you kidding?" he said.

5

"We're lucky if we aren't all alone in this place. We have fewer tourists every year. The only ones we get these days are the ones who get lost."

Boulder Bay used to get a lot of vacationers. They'd stay at the Boulder Bay Inn, which Josh's family owns, or they'd rent a house down by the beach. For a few months in the summer, the town's three restaurants would be full most nights, and the shops along Bay Street would be crowded with strangers.

But those days were over. Boulder Bay was too out-of-the-way, now that the new highway cut through to Birch Point twelve miles north of us. Why would anyone want to spend an hour on our winding narrow roads just to end up in Boulder Bay?

I looked over at the sandwich on the kitchen table. I was really hungry. And after the sandwich, I was hoping to take a nap. "I don't know," I told Josh over the phone. "I'm kind of busy at the moment."

"Busy?" Josh sputtered. "This is summer. How can you be busy?"

I looked at my sandwich and tried to think of an excuse. "I thought I might help my dad around here," I said. "There's tons of stuff that needs to be done while the weather's good."

"Yeah, right," Josh scoffed. "Like your dad needs any help. He has the world's easiest job: when it gets dark, he turns on a light. Most of us do that every night for free."

I sighed loudly into the phone. "You *know* it's a lot more complicated than that," I told him. "And what is it you want me to see anyway?"

"It's a movie," he told me. "You're never going to believe it."

"What kind of movie?"

"A dumb monster movie," he said.

"Why would I want to come all the way into town for that?"

"Trust me," Josh said. "It's worth it. If you aren't glad you came, I'll refund your money."

I looked out the kitchen window at the calm water of the bay. It was overcast and breezy, but I'd be fine heading across in my skiff.

"So this movie is pretty good?" I asked.

Josh laughed. "No, it's absolutely terrible," he said. "You'll never see a worse movie. But there's something very special about it. Believe me, you won't be disappointed."

I sighed again. "OK," I said. "Meet me at the marina in half an hour. This had better be good."

It was pretty cold out on the bay, but I had my warmest jacket on, and I had the hood pulled up over my head. The marina was at the farthest end of the bay, where the water is sheltered and always calm. I usually keep pretty close to the shore and leave the deeper water of the bay for the bigger boats, but there weren't many out today, so I cut straight across to save some time.

When I got close to the marina, I saw Josh standing on the dock waving at me with both arms, like he was afraid I was going to miss him. I waved back at him so he'd stop.

A lot of the fishing boats were tied to their moorings in the marina. It had been a bad year for the fishermen so far, and I knew some of them were wondering how they were going to survive the summer.

I slowed the engine and pulled up beside the public dock. I tossed Josh a rope, and he tied my skiff to the dock with an awkward knot.

"I would have recommended a clove hitch," I told him as I climbed up on the dock. "But your retardo hitch will probably do."

Josh looked down at the lumpy knot he'd just tied and shrugged. "What do I need to know knots for?" he asked me. "I hate boats. All I ever tie are my shoelaces."

A fishing boat chugged by us into the marina. My friend Pete stood on the deck looking down at the water and stroking his red beard. "Any luck?" I called up to him as he passed.

He shook his head gravely. "Out three days and all I caught was a cold."

His shipmate, Jeff, waved from the cabin window. "Storm coming ashore," he reported. I looked at the line of gray clouds on the horizon. He was right.

"Come on," Josh said. "You can talk to those guys on your own time. We've got a movie to catch."

Before the movie started, Josh bought a bucket of popcorn, and I bought some Raisinettes. The lights had already been dimmed when we made our way to our seats. It was hard to see in the dark, but I was pretty sure we were the only two people in the theater. It made me wonder if the movie went on automatically, even if no one was there to watch it.

Josh led me to two seats right in the middle of the theater, and we sat down. A few years ago, this theater would have seen quite a bit of business during the summer. And it would have shown all the first-run summer blockbusters. But the tourism was gone, and now the fishing was gone too. The theater showed only old movies, and not many people came to see them. No one was doing very well in Boulder Bay.

We sat through a couple of coming attractions, and my eyes adjusted to the darkness. I looked around. We *were* the only people here. It was kind of cool and kind of depressing at the same time.

Some spooky music started to play. At first it sounded like it was being played underwater, and the picture on the screen stuttered and skipped. But then the film seemed to catch in the sprockets, and everything became normal. The words on the screen said: A VICTOR VANCE FILM.

The screen went black again, and the first thing I saw was a dark, stormy sky. Lightning flickered among huge gray clouds. Rain blew across dark choppy water. Waves crashed against rocks.

I could feel Josh watching me in the dark.

Next I saw a small town in a heavy rainstorm. Houses and little stores huddled in the darkness— their dimly lit windows glimmered behind a blowing curtain of rain. The camera moved down the wet street, passing building after building.

Josh kept watching me. It was getting on my nerves.

On the movie screen I saw a small bay. A sudden bolt of lightning struck the water in the cove. And then I saw a lighthouse, its beacon glimmering through the driving rain.

That's when it hit me.

It was *my* lighthouse in the movie. It was *our* town.

"Hey, that's the lighthouse," I said. "That's *my* lighthouse."

"Amazing powers of recognition," Josh told me. "Especially since you've only lived in it for thirteen years."

"So it was filmed here?" I said. "This movie was made right here in town?"

"Another dazzling mental feat," Josh teased. "You never cease to amaze me."

I leaned forward and stared at the screen—the tiny lighthouse out on the point turned its light through the pouring rain. I'd never realized how isolated and lonely it looked. Was it just a trick of the camera?

Blaring music came on suddenly, and the words TERROR COVE filled the screen.

"That lightning strike in the bay brought the monster out of hibernation," Josh explained in a whisper—although, of course, there wasn't a single other person in the theater to hear him.

11

"I imagine that kind of thing happens all the time," I said in my normal speaking voice.

Josh laughed. "Yeah," he said, more loudly now. "I hear monsters are very light sleepers."

A VICTOR VANCE PRODUCTION, the words on the screen said. I didn't know who Victor Vance was, but his name kept coming up in the credits. He was the creator, writer, director, and executive producer—and a few other things I'd never heard of before.

To be honest, his movie was really bad. It looked like it was made in the '70s, and everyone had funny-looking haircuts and shirts with big collars. The acting was terrible, and the special effects were even worse. But Josh was right: It was cool to see our little town in a movie—even if it *was* about some kind of cheapo sea monster.

The monster looked like a giant octopus with long snaking tentacles. It also had an undulating, scaly body like a sea serpent and a head like a pterodactyl. It looked like they had taken different monsters from a bunch of earlier movies and stitched them all together to save money. When the light hit it right, you could see the wires that made it move.

Every time there was a big storm, the monster would come up from the bottom of the bay to attack people. In one of the first scenes, it crawled up Bay Street, where my friend Jeffrey Pruner lives.

"There's the bait shop," Josh told me, as the monster passed a small waterfront building. "And there's the entrance to the marina." He was right—although neither one looked much the way they did today. The monster passed a few houses and then went through a gate and up toward one of the homes.

"Isn't that Jeffrey's house?" I asked Josh.

"It's not the right color," Josh said.

"I know," I said. "But this was filmed a long time ago. It has probably been repainted since then. Look, that's his front porch, isn't it?"

"Watch out, Jeffrey!" Josh yelled at the screen, half laughing. "It's coming. Run for your life!"

"Call Officer Borders!" I yelled. "Call the FBI! Call the CIA!"

"Call the IRS!" Josh yelled. "Call PBS!"

"Call the whole alphabet!" I yelled. "It's a pretty big monster."

The monster smashed one of the windows on Jeffrey's house and squeezed its rubbery body through. The scene that followed was too dark to see much, but there was plenty of screaming and the sounds of things being smashed. Finally the monster slipped back out the window and slid into the bay again. The next morning, everyone in the house was missing.

"Poor Jeffrey," Josh said. "He's octopus food."

"It's tragic," I said. "When I saw him yesterday, he was so full of life."

The next scene showed the exterior of a university, but it was really just the backside of the grocery store with a big sign over the door that read Terror Cove State University. Then it showed a professor in his lab. He wore round glasses, and his hair looked like he had just taken a long ride in a convertible. There were all kinds of bubbling test tubes and electrical gizmos all over the place.

"I always thought this was such a boring town," I told Josh, while the professor on the screen fiddled with test tubes and Bunsen burners. "But if we really had some kind of monster, it wouldn't be so bad."

The professor was doing experiments on a large pulsing blob; it was supposed to be a monster egg that local fishermen had caught in a net. The egg was purple and slimy and seemed to glow from the inside. The professor hooked it up to some sparking wires.

"What's he trying to do?" I asked Josh.

"I'm pretty sure he's making an omelette," Josh told me.

In the next scene, some boys were at the end of the pier fishing—in the middle of a downpour, of course! It was all foggy, and they were huddled together talking about girls and listening to a radio, which for some reason kept playing music, even though water was pouring all over it.

"Fishing in the rain!" Josh scoffed. "How stupid do they think we are? Everyone knows fish don't like wet weather!" I laughed again. I was having a great time making fun of this stupid movie.

Some other kid was supposed to meet the boys at the end of the pier, so when they heard a noise behind them in the thick fog, they thought it was their friend. But, of course it wasn't—and the creature ate them all while the radio played "Monster Mash." After the monster slipped back into the bay, the last kid showed up and found the abandoned fishing rods and radio.

"Why would anyone call their town Terror Cove?" Josh wondered aloud in the dark. "Seems like monsters would just flock to a place like that."

"Yeah," I said. "After all, they called *this* place Boulder Bay—and the next thing you know it's full of big rocks."

"This is what I'm saying," Josh agreed.

The next morning, the professor found some green slimy stuff on the pier railing when he was taking a walk. He put it in a test tube and took it back to his laboratory at the grocery store.

In the following scene, a man and a woman were on a big yacht. A huge storm was coming in, and they were trying to get back to the marina before it hit. It was late at night, and the waves on the bay were tossing the boat all over the place. The couple kept talking about "the kitchen" and "the floor"—when anyone who's owned a boat would say "the galley" and "the deck." It was really pretty funny.

Finally the engine broke down in the middle of the bay. The man told the woman to "take the steering wheel" so he could go out and check on the engine. While he was standing at the stern of the boat tightening something with a wrench, a giant tentacle wrapped around his ankles. There was a long and clumsy struggle, and finally the monster pulled him overboard. It was supposed to be scary, but it was hard not to laugh at the terrible acting and the dumb special effects.

The woman inside at the "steering wheel" kept calling for her husband. She started to get hysterical. Instead of getting on the radio and calling the Coast Guard, she grabbed a giant butcher knife from "the kitchen" and headed out through the cabin door.

"Taking a butcher knife out in the middle of a storm on a slippery, rolling deck," I said. *"That's good thinking."*

"Yeah," Josh said. "A steel knife like that—she could get struck by lightning."

I laughed. The lady searched the deck for her husband, and when she heard a splashing in the water, she crouched over the boat's railing and peered down into the waves. Of course, a tentacle rocketed up at her and wrapped around her neck. She stabbed at it with the butcher knife, and it oozed green slime before it let go. She dropped the knife and ran back to the bright cabin—but of course she didn't even bother to close the door behind her.

"Oh, no," Josh said dramatically. "You leave a door open like that at night and bugs get in." I laughed again.

The monster cornered her and dragged her, screaming, into the ocean.

Back at the grocery store, the professor assembled a reverse proton laser beam—some kind of ray gun he built especially for killing sea monsters.

The next time a storm blew in, he climbed the tower of the lighthouse with his ray gun so he'd have a commanding view of the bay.

"I told Mom she shouldn't leave a key under the mat," I said. "Professors are always sneaking into lighthouses like that."

Of course, the monster saw the professor up there. The creature climbed the tower of the lighthouse trying to get at the professor, who was taking forever to set up his reverse proton laser beam. (It was a small model of a lighthouse that looked nothing like ours, and what looked like a hand puppet version of the monster.)

The professor got the laser working just in time and aimed the reverse proton beam down at the monster just before it smothered the light with its long rubber tentacle. There was a giant explosion, and when the smoke cleared, the professor and the monster were both gone.

In the final scene, a new professor took over the lab. Of course, he didn't know what the monster egg was, so he threw it in the trash can. That night, of course, a storm blew in, and a tiny version of the same monster oozed out of the Dumpster. It slithered through town in the rain and disappeared into the bay, with the lighthouse in the distance shining its light through the rain.

"*It's out there!*" I screeched in mock terror while the music blared and the credits rolled. "It's been biding its time all these years just waiting for an excuse to *eat us all!*"

"And I'd say it's pretty hungry by this time."

When the lights in the theater came up, Josh had tears in his eyes he was laughing so hard. "Wasn't that a riot?" he asked me. "It figures that if they were going to make a movie in this stupid town, it would be one as bad as that!"

Chapter 2

I stood under the marquee while the rain came down in sheets. There was no way to get back across the bay in my skiff in such rough weather, so I'd called my mom from the theater lobby and asked her to pick me up. I'd have to walk into town tomorrow when the storm cleared and take the skiff back out to Lighthouse Point.

Josh lived just down Clark Street, so he told me good-bye and took off running through the rain toward home, holding his jacket over his head.

I hadn't seen anyone go into the theater for the next showing of *Terror Cove,* and I wondered if the movie was playing in there now to a house full of empty seats. I glanced at my watch. Mom was taking her time.

The streetlights on Clark Street were dim and blurry behind the rain. Each time a car hissed by on the flooded street, its windshield wipers flipping back and forth, I hoped it was Mom coming to pick me up. The sight of the lit windows along the street and the smell of firewood in the air made me feel even colder. At least I was dry under the overhang of the theater's marquee. I watched the rain spatter on the sidewalk in front of me. Wasn't this the same sidewalk the baby monster had slithered down in the last scene of the movie—in a storm just like this one? I chuckled to myself. What a lame movie!

I pulled my jacket tighter around me and dug my cold hands deep in the pockets. It was a miserable night to be outside waiting for a ride, and Mom sure was taking a long time. When I looked up, a pair of blurry yellow lights turned onto Clark Street, and in a few seconds, Mom's car pulled up to the curb in front of me.

She reached across and unlocked the passenger side door. I glanced up quickly at the falling rain and then jogged across the slippery pavement. I pulled open the door and slid inside, dripping all over Mom's upholstery. How did I get so wet in the few seconds it took me to get in the car?

"You must be freezing," Mom said. "Sorry it took me so long. Are you OK?"

The car's heater blew hot air over my feet and legs. I leaned forward and felt the rising air on my face. "I'm fine," I said. "Just a little cold is all."

"You should have checked with Dad before taking the skiff out on a day like this," she said. As a lighthouse keeper, Dad always got the latest weather reports.

"I know," I said. "But the weather looked fine a couple of hours ago."

We headed down Clark Street to the base of the dock and turned right. As we passed the dock, I pressed my face against the window to see if the skiff was OK—after all, it had been tied up with one of Josh's retardo hitches—but all I could see was darkness and rain. I wasn't really worried. Pete would keep an eye on it.

The car labored up the steep road that mounted the high rocky ledge to the north of town. Up ahead, the lighthouse's lonely beacon swept through the heavy rain. Behind us I could see the dim lights of town. We came to the big curve at the top of the cliff, and Mom slowed the car nearly to a stop so we wouldn't slide on the slick road.

Suddenly the dark bay was spread out below us—just like in the first scene of the movie. This was probably the very spot where they'd put the camera all those years ago.

I peered down at the cove. A huge bolt of lightning suddenly struck the middle of the bay, lighting up the churning water for an instant. I jumped.

"What's the matter, honey?" Mom asked. "Are you feeling a little nervous?"

I laughed at myself and shook my head. "That looked exactly like the first scene of the movie we just saw," I told her. "It was a dumb monster movie, but it was pretty cool. They filmed it right here in town."

"Uh-huh," Mom said. I could tell she wasn't really listening. Her mind was on the slick, curving road.

"Monsters are notoriously light sleepers," I told her.

"That's nice, honey," Mom said. I smiled and lay my head back on the seat. It felt good to be warm again.

We finally crested the cliff, and I saw the lighthouse out on the point again. Though I couldn't hear it yet, I knew the foghorn was sending its deep moan out over the turbulent waves. With that and the rain hammering on the roof, I knew it would be hard to sleep tonight.

By noon the next day the sky had cleared and the sun was out. I checked with Dad. He said he expected fair weather for the next few days, which was good news if I was going to get my skiff back safely. I put on my jacket and went out on the doorstep with Dad's most powerful binoculars. I stood there looking across the water at the town of Boulder Bay.

A few sailboats were out on the bay, now that the weather had improved. I could make out a few people fishing from the end of the public dock at the marina, and my skiff was still tied up and afloat. It would be a long walk into town, so the sooner I set out, the sooner I'd have my skiff back. I went inside and put the binoculars back in their drawer.

I found Mom and told her where I was going. I headed up the drive on foot. The ground was soft and full of puddles, and everything had that rain-on-grass smell. I reached the highway and started walking along the shoulder toward town, hoping someone I knew would happen by and offer me a ride.

I was on Bay Street, close to the dock, when I thought of telling Jeffrey about the movie Josh and I had seen the day before. I knew he'd get a kick out of it, especially since his house was the site of the first monster attack. By tomorrow a new movie would be in the theater; if Jeffrey was going to see it, it would have to be today.

As I passed the dock, I looked over to make sure my skiff was still OK. A group of older kids was fishing off the end of the dock. It seemed pretty pointless to me—especially since the professional fishermen like Pete and Jeff, with their big nets and all their fancy equipment, were hardly catching anything.

When I finally got to Jeffrey's house, it looked pretty beat up by the storm. The two family cars parked out front were splattered with mud and plastered with limp, fallen leaves. The houses on Bay Street always got the worst of it when a storm blew in from the ocean.

The front gate in Jeffrey's white picket fence was open. It hung at an odd angle, with one corner stuck in the mud, as if the top hinge had broken in the storm. Some shingles had come loose from the roof and lay scattered about the puddled lawn.

I passed through the broken gate and walked up the front path. A large branch from the maple tree in the front yard had fallen during the storm. It lay at an angle across the lawn and partly covered the muddy front path. On one end, the yellow wood curled like frayed rope. I looked down at the tangle of leaves and twigs. I was surprised Mr. Pruner, Jeffrey's dad, hadn't cut it up with his chain saw yet. He was very particular about his garden.

I glanced at the houses on either side. It was strange, but it seemed like the storm had hit Jeffrey's house much harder than the other two. I stepped over the fallen branch and crossed the front porch. I grabbed the big brass knocker on the front door and banged it a couple of times.

There was no answer.

I banged harder and then pressed my ear to the door. There was no sound inside, not even the usual barking of their Scottish terrier.

I went down the porch steps and stood in the front yard looking up at Jeffrey's window. "Jeffrey?" I called. "You in there?"

Again, there was no answer. They'd all gone somewhere. But how? Both their cars were parked out front. I looked around. Wind off the bay rustled the branches above my head. Water dripped somewhere. Suddenly I got a sinking feeling in my stomach.

I thought of *Terror Cove*. I pictured a huge monster heaving out of the water and oozing through the storm toward this very house, lightning flashes lighting up its glistening rubbery body. I felt a chill run up my spine, but I shrugged it off. I was acting like an idiot.

"Jeffrey Pruner," I called at the house. "Are you in there? It's me—Danny Dolan."

Still, no one answered. I turned and headed back down the path and out the gate, but instead of leaving, I just stood on the sidewalk in front of Jeffrey's house, looking out at the pier and the rest of Boulder Bay. The sky was slate colored, and the water was choppy.

I looked down Bay Street. Again I pictured that huge slimy monster oozing its way up the hill. I pictured a long tentacle curling around the lamppost and the long, eel-like body pulling itself over the crest of the hill. It was strange: the movie hadn't been scary when I was watching it—just kind of goofy. But now, a day later—in broad daylight—it was giving me the heebie jeebies. Wasn't it supposed to be the other way around?

I went back through the gate into Jeffrey's yard again, but instead of going up to the porch, I went around the side.

Then I saw it.

The big kitchen window on the side of the house was smashed in. I went over, stood on my tiptoes, and peeked inside, careful not to cut my fingers on the broken glass.

The kitchen was a mess. Broken glass was scattered everywhere. The walls were spattered with mud, and brown water stood in a big pool on the floor. A chair from the kitchen table lay propped against the counter as if it had been knocked over. One of the cupboard doors lay open, and its contents were strewn across the counter and the floor.

I took a sudden step away from the window— as if I had heard a big dog bark inside. The small hairs on the back of my neck began to quiver, and I felt a rush of adrenaline. What had happened here? Where was Jeffrey? Where was his family? Where was his Scottish terrier?

I didn't know what to do. I had to tell someone. I jogged toward the gate, glancing over my shoulder as I ran—my heart pounding. I nearly tripped over the fallen branch. I burst through the front gate and ran up Bay Street.

When I got to the Town Hall, my side was aching, and I was gasping for air. I ran up the front steps, through the lobby, and down the back hallway. I burst through the door marked Boulder Bay Police.

In the front room, Mrs. Borders looked up from

her knitting. "What is it?" she wanted to know. "What's the matter?"

"It's the Pruners," I told her, gasping for air. "Something's happened to the Pruners."

"Randall," Mrs. Borders called into the next office. "There's someone here to see you, Randall."

Randall Borders was Boulder Bay's only full-time policeman. He'd left town for college when I was a little kid, and when he came back, they'd put him in charge of law enforcement. Sometimes in the summer he'd hire a few part-time deputies. His mother, Mrs. Borders, called herself the dispatcher, but she didn't get paid, and the town didn't have a police radio for her to dispatch on. She mostly sat in the office and knitted, and yelled through the door to her son when anyone showed up to see him.

"Randall?" she called again, an edge in her voice now. "Answer me when I talk to you."

"Coming, Mother," Officer Borders called.

When he came out of his office, he was buckling his utility belt. He saw me and nodded hello.

"What seems to be the problem, Danny?" He stood in front of me, arms folded, feet spread wide apart.

"Something's happened to the Pruners," I said. "Their house is empty. The side window is broken."

He stroked his square chin. "Does it look like a robbery?"

"Maybe," I said. "Maybe it was just the storm." I swallowed. "Maybe it was something else."

"Well, let's go check it out," Officer Borders said. I followed him to the door.

"Remember to wear your jacket," Mrs. Borders said. "It's cold outside."

I waited in the doorway while Officer Borders went back in his office for his jacket.

When we pulled up in front of the Pruners' house in the police cruiser, Officer Borders let out a whistle. Everything was just as I had left it, and it was a big mess.

"Looks almost like a tornado touched down here," he said, and it wasn't far from the truth. "I didn't think last night's storm would have done *this* much damage."

"But just this one house," I said. "The others look fine. Isn't that kind of weird?"

Officer Borders didn't answer. He just opened the door of the cruiser and got out. He strode over to the broken gate. I struggled with the passenger door and finally got out. I jogged to catch up with him. We stepped over the fallen branch and went across the porch to the front door. Officer Borders hammered on the door with the side of his fist. "Anyone home?" he called. There was no answer. He banged on the door again.

"Both their cars are here," I told him. "They're the ones parked right out front."

He glanced over at them and banged on the door again. When no one answered, Officer Borders asked me to show him the broken window. I led him across the spongy lawn to the side of the house.

Officer Borders studied the broken window in silence. He leaned inside, careful not to cut himself on the jagged pieces of glass still jutting from the window frame.

"It was definitely smashed from the outside," he said. "All the broken glass is in there."

"What do you think happened?" I asked him.

"Probably the storm," he said. "But it's pretty weird."

"Weird how?"

"Well, nothing else on the side of the house is damaged," he said. "I'd expect the windows out front to be broken—the ones facing the bay. That's where the storm came from."

I followed Officer Borders around to the front of the house. I thought he was going to the front door, but instead he turned up the front path and stepped over the fallen branch again. He seemed to be leaving.

I stood in front of the porch watching him. "Where are you going?" I asked him.

He turned to look at me. "Back to the station," he told me. "Come on. I'll give you a ride."

"Aren't you going to go inside?" I asked him. "Aren't you going to make sure everything's OK?"

"Everything *is* OK," Officer Borders told me. "When they get back they'll find a broken window. I'm not going to break down the door as well." He walked over to the parked police cruiser. I jogged after him.

"But they didn't go anywhere," I told him, coming out the gate. "Their cars are right here."

Officer Borders shrugged and opened the car door. "Maybe someone picked them up," he said. "Maybe they took a taxi to the airport in Birch Point. They're not here, so they must have gone somewhere."

"I talked to Jeffrey a couple of days ago," I told him. Officer Borders and I were standing on either side of the car now, talking over the roof. "He didn't say anything about going anywhere."

"This is a free country," Officer Borders reminded me. "You don't have to tell anyone what you're doing or where you're going." He looked at me a long time. "Look, if you think something's happened here, why don't you tell me what it is?"

I didn't know what to say. I sure wasn't going to tell him what I was thinking. If I told him some kind of slimy monster from the deep had slid in Jeffrey's kitchen window and eaten the Pruner family, he'd think I was nuts. And maybe I was. But, still, I couldn't think of any *other* explanation at the moment. I sighed. Officer Borders was probably right. "I guess they just went some-where," I said, more to myself than to him. "And the storm broke their window."

Officer Borders nodded. "Come on," he said. "Get in. If it will make you feel any better, we can go by Hank's Hardware Store. Maybe Hank can come over and nail up some plywood so no more rain gets in." He sat down in the car and pulled the door shut.

I glanced up at Jeffrey's house again and then pulled open the passenger door.

Chapter 3

Normally, it would have been kind of cool riding around town in the police cruiser with Officer Borders, but all I could think about was Jeffrey Pruner and his missing family.

I looked out the window as we drove. The streets were still wet from the rain the night before. We passed the entrance to the marina and the bait shop. The wheels of the cruiser hissed on the wet asphalt. We turned up Clark Street, and as we passed by the different shops and houses, I remembered how the baby monster had oozed its way down this same street on its way to the ocean in the final scene of the movie.

Up ahead, I saw the theater. The words TERROR COVE still looked down on us from the marquee. By tomorrow some other old movie would be playing, and the words would be gone, but what if the monster stayed on after the movie left town?

At the end of Clark Street we came to the Boulder Bay Inn, where Josh lived.

"Hey," I asked Officer Borders, "could you drop me off here?"

Officer Borders pulled the police car over to the curb. I opened the door.

"Thanks for reporting the broken window," Officer Borders told me. "There could have been a lot of water damage to the Pruners' house when the next storm came through."

"Sure thing," I said. "Thanks for coming to check it out."

I slammed the door of the police car. Officer Borders leaned over and rolled down the window. "Say," he said. "If you hear from your friend, Jeffrey, be sure to let me know."

Why did he want me to do that? I wondered. Was he suspicious about something? "OK," I told him. "I'll let you know when I hear from him."

The police car pulled away. I just stood there watching it. The brake lights came on as he slowed to turn the corner. When the cruiser was out of sight, I turned and climbed the steps to the Boulder Bay Inn.

The inn was the largest building in town, with windowed dormers jutting from the roof and a round tower in one corner. It was three stories high, had both front and back stairs and about a dozen fireplaces. It was ideal for an inn, but few people came by Boulder Bay anymore. Josh's family was in as dire straits as everyone else in town.

I pushed open the door and went inside. A bell jangled above my head. The long, wood-paneled lobby was pretty dark. After being out in the sun and the rain-gleaming streets, it took a moment for my eyes to adjust. No one was in the lobby, but a cozy fire crackled in the grate. I pushed the door shut behind me, and the bell jangled again.

"May I help you?" a piping voice asked. I jumped a little—I was still a bit on edge. I glanced toward the front desk, where the voice had come from. No one was there.

"Hello?" I said nervously. "Did I just hear a voice?"

"What do *you* think?" the voice said again.

I went to the desk and stood on my tiptoes to lean over it. Josh's little sister, Jessica, was back there—too short to be seen from the other side. She was rummaging in one of the cupboards.

"Hey, Jess," I said. "Did you pull desk duty today?"

"Nah," she said, slamming one cupboard door and opening the next. "Nobody's working desk today. We don't have any guests, and there are no reservations until the weekend. I'm just looking for my left shoe. I was going to go outside."

I looked down at her feet. Sure enough, she was wearing only one white sneaker. I laughed. Jessica was always looking for something. Josh claimed that his little sister was a gateway to another dimension. Everything she touched seemed to disappear and eventually turn up someplace completely impossible—like the time she lost her calculator, and it turned up three months later in the back of the freezer.

"Shoes, huh?" I glanced around behind the desk. "Have you looked in the file cabinet under *S?*" I asked her. "Or would it be filed under *L* for '*left* shoe'?"

Jessica closed the cupboard door, straightened up, and turned to look at me. She put her hands on her hips and cocked her head to one side. "Why don't you just file yourself under *N* for 'not funny'?" she suggested. She got down on all fours and began to root around under the counter.

"Is Josh here?" I asked her. "I really need to talk to him." She either didn't hear me or just ignored me.

"It's got to be around here somewhere," she said.

"When was the last time you remember seeing it?" I asked her.

"Up in my room last night," she said, her voice muffled by the counter.

"Did you come down here since then?"

"Nope," she said.

I shook my head. She was pathetic. "Well, then *why* are you looking down here?" I asked. "It doesn't make any sense."

Jessica didn't answer me. She just kept noisily rummaging around under the desk.

"This is stupid," I told her, straining to lean farther over the counter. "You're wasting your time. This is the *last* place it would be." It was hopeless. There was no talking to her. "So is Josh here or not?"

"Found it!" she cried. She straightened up, red-faced from exertion, and triumphantly held her white sneaker up for me to see. A loose strand of hair hung down in front of her face, and she puffed it out of the way.

"If it was up in your room last night, how did it end up down here?"

"Beats me," she said airily as she plopped down on the ground and pulled on the shoe.

"It doesn't make any sense," I told her. "You just forgot. You *had* to have come down here last night. That shoe didn't just hop down the stairs on its own."

"Look, Josh is upstairs," she told me, tying her shoelace. "Why don't you go bother *him* instead of heckling *me* all the time?"

I sighed and started up the staircase. Jessica headed outside. When I got to the second-floor landing, I heard the front door slam.

The second floor was eerily silent. Josh and his family lived on the third floor. All the rooms on the second floor were reserved for paying guests, and—like Jessica said—there weren't any.

I went down the silent hallway and climbed the second flight of stairs. I knocked on Josh's door.

"Go *away*, Jessica," he called through the closed door. "I haven't got your stupid shoe."

"She found it," I called back. "It was at my house."

Josh laughed. "Come in," he said. "I didn't know it was you."

I pushed the door open. Josh lay on his bed reading a book. He marked his place and set the book on his bedside table.

"You come into town to get your boat?" he said.

"It's a skiff," I told him for the umpteenth time. "Yeah, I did, but the weirdest thing happened."

Josh sat up on the edge of his bed. "What?" he asked. "What happened?"

I pulled the chair away from Josh's desk and sat down on it backwards so I was facing him. I didn't know where to begin. How do you tell your best friend what you're thinking, when what you're thinking sounds stupid even to you?

"Remember that dumb movie we saw yesterday?" I asked him.

"Yeah."

"Well, last night, when Mom was driving me home, the lightning struck the water just like in the first scene of the movie. You know, when the monster woke up from his hibernation."

"Yeah, so?"

I hugged the back of the chair and tried to think of how to put my worry into words. How do you tell someone that there just might be a monster in town?

"OK," I said. "You're probably going to make fun of me for the rest of my life for this, but here's what I'm thinking." I told Josh everything that had happened—the broken window at Jeffrey's house, the cars parked outside, my ride with Officer Borders. Josh didn't say anything. He just sat there smiling at me—his grin growing bigger with every sentence I said.

When I was done, he fell back on his bed laughing. "OK," I said. "I know it's a little weird, but you've got to admit it's a bizarre coincidence."

"So you're saying that Son of the Slime Monster has come back to finish the work his father began?" Josh said. "Danny, do you have any idea how stupid that is? That was a monster movie we were watching, not a documentary."

Actually, I had a pretty good idea how stupid it was. He didn't have to tell me that. But I could still feel the hair on my arms standing on end as I thought about it. The whole thing gave me the creeps.

I looked at Josh. He was sitting up on his bed again, but he was still grinning at me.

I fidgeted on my chair and looked down at the floor. "It's just kind of spooky is all," I told him, feeling a little defensive. "Doesn't it strike you as weird that Jeffrey and his whole family disappeared just like in the movie?"

"No," Josh said. "I'm surprised more people don't disappear from this stupid town. I'd do it myself if I got the chance."

I shook my head. "People *don't* just disappear," I reasoned.

"OK," Josh said. "They didn't *disappear*. That's too dramatic a word. They just *went* somewhere. Maybe they're on vacation."

"Yeah, if they were *hitchhiking*," I said. "All their cars are parked outside the house, and Jeffrey didn't say anything to me about going on vacation."

"Maybe someone picked them up," Josh said. "Maybe someone drove them to the train station. There are hundreds of plausible explanations— and none of them involve monsters."

"OK," I said. "OK. You win. There's no monster. I'm just thinking out loud is all."

"Well *stop* thinking," Josh said. "There's nothing to worry about. Jeffrey is probably up in Birch Point right now walking along the boardwalk eating ice cream."

He was right. I knew it. I had to laugh. It was such a stupid idea. "You're right," I said. "I guess we don't need to worry until a group of kids disappear from the end of the dock."

Josh laughed. "If they go fishing in a rain storm, they're just asking for it," he said.

As if on cue, there was a knock on Josh's door. "You guys in there?" Jessica's piping voice asked.

"Just go away," Josh called through the door. "We're talking in here."

"You guys want to go fishing?" Jessica's voice asked hopefully.

Josh grinned at me. "Fishing?" he said. He went over and opened the door. There stood Jessica, a bucket in one hand, the other hand wrapped around four graphite fishing rods that clattered each time she moved. I wondered how she'd knocked on the door.

"You going fishing on the pier?" Josh asked her. He turned and grinned at me. "Hey," he said. "This is my big chance."

"It's not raining," I reminded him.

"With any luck he'll be too hungry to wait," Josh said.

"What are you guys talking about?" Jessica wanted to know. "You want to come or not?"

"Only if *you're* the bait," Josh said.

"Come on, you guys," Jessica said. "It'll be great. We can call Bonnie."

"Bonnie the Vegetarian will only come if we're fishing for carrots," I reminded her.

"Well then, just the three of us," Jessica said. "I'll lend you one of my rods." She held the fist full of rods up for us to see.

"Where did you get those?" Josh asked her. "I thought you *lost* all your fishing gear."

"I did," she said. "But I found some new ones."

"You *found* those?" Josh tilted his head and looked at the fancy fishing rods.

"Yeah," Jessica said. "They were sitting at the end of the dock just now. Someone must have left them there last night. I'm surprised they didn't get washed off the dock in the storm."

"I saw some kids fishing there this morning," I said.

"Well, they're gone now," Jessica replied. "The dock's totally abandoned." She gripped the rods together, as if we might try to take them. "Finders keepers."

A chill crept up the back of my neck. Josh's mouth fell open. Four abandoned fishing rods at the end of the dock? I felt a sudden weight on my chest that made it difficult to breathe. Josh looked at me wide-eyed.

I stood up. "OK," I said. "It's officially time to worry."

Down at the dock, we walked right past my skiff and on to the end where Jessica said she found the four abandoned fishing rods propped up against the railing.

"They were right here," she said. "The lines were still in the water. But no one was around. I looked all over for the owners."

Josh looked at me. "It doesn't prove anything," he said. He sounded like he was trying to convince himself. "It's just some fishing rods."

"What are you guys talking about?" Jessica wanted to know.

I ignored her. "I know it's just some fishing rods," I said to Josh. "But it's still another weird coincidence."

"They are nice rods," Josh admitted. "And those reels are brand new. I can't imagine anyone just walking away and leaving them here."

"Look, what is your problem?" Jessica asked. "Are we going to fish or not?"

We still ignored her. I leaned over the dock railing and looked down into the water—half expecting to see some kind of monster parked there. But all I saw was my own reflection looking back up at me from the shimmering green water.

"OK, tell me straight," I said. "Do you have the willies or what?"

"Hel-*lo*," Jessica said. "What's going on here?"

"What happened next in the movie?" Josh asked.

"You should know," I said. "You're the one who saw it twice."

"Didn't the monster attack those people on the yacht?" he asked.

"Monster?" Jessica said. We ignored her.

"Yeah," I said. "But first the professor guy found that green slimy stuff on the dock. Maybe we should look around."

We did. Even Jessica helped, though she had no idea what we were looking for. "Is this it?" she asked, holding up a rusty penknife that she'd found wedged in a crack.

"No," Josh snapped. "We're not looking for a knife."

Jessica looked at the knife more closely. "Hey, this is *mine!*" she said. "I thought it was in my desk."

Josh just rolled his eyes and kept looking. We found nothing. No green slime. No suction-cup prints. No anything.

I had a knot in my stomach. What was going on here? If there was a monster in town, we needed to tell someone. But there was no point in telling anyone until we were sure. I looked over at Jessica. She was trying to pry open the rusty penknife. Her tongue poked out of the corner of her mouth as she concentrated.

I pulled Josh aside so Jessica couldn't hear us. "Look," I said. "We've got to find out what's going on here."

"Agreed," he said. "But how do we do that?"

"How should I know?" I said. "Do I *look* like a professor?"

Josh thought about it a moment, and then his face lit up. I could practically see the light bulb above his head. "I've got an idea," he said. "In the movie the monster always came out on the bay when there was an electrical storm, right?"

"Right."

"And we can see the whole bay from up on Lighthouse Point, right?"

"Right."

"So next time there's a big storm, I'll come over and spend the night," Josh said. "We can see the whole bay from your bedroom window. We can watch it all through the storm, and that'll *prove* there's no monster out there."

I thought about it. It seemed like a pretty good idea. "OK," I said. "You come over the next time there's a storm, and we'll stay up all night—which I usually do anyway because you snore so loudly."

I looked over at Jessica. She was baiting a hook with a lump of squid.

"It's settled then," I said. "The next stormy night, we keep an all-night monster watch."

"And when the monster doesn't show, we'll have a good laugh at your expense," Josh said.

I went over to where my skiff was tied up and climbed down into it. I stood there a moment, one hand on the dock, the skiff rocking beneath my feet. I looked down at the green water between the skiff and the dock. Who knew what was down there? I didn't really want to be on the water right then, but I didn't want Josh to think I was scared. I untied the line that held my skiff to the dock and sat down in the stern.

"You guys want to come with me?" I asked them. The skiff drifted a few feet from the dock. "My mom can drive you back into town tonight. You can have dinner with us." I don't know why I asked; Josh hated boating, and Jessica was already lowering her baited line into the water on the other side of the dock.

"Not this time," Josh said, shielding the morning sun from his eyes with his hand. He'd never admit it, but I think he's scared of the water. He'd never been in my skiff in his life. "Maybe later."

I started up the motor and steered away from the dock. "See ya," I yelled back at Josh, trying to sound chipper. "I'll call you when I check Dad's weather reports."

Josh waved and called something I couldn't make out. A moment later I was out on the deep and choppy water of the bay. The lighthouse, far out on the point, seemed much farther away than it should have been.

At moments like this, I try to think of my favorite Bible story. It's about the guy I'm named after—Daniel. When he was thrown in the lions' den, God shut the lions' mouths so they couldn't harm him. I looked down at the green water and prayed that God would do the same for me.

Chapter 4

The next storm rolled in off the ocean three days later. Josh asked his mom if he could come out to the lighthouse and spend the night. About an hour before dinner, Josh's mom pulled up next to the lighthouse in her minivan. I went out on the front steps and waved. It wasn't raining yet, but the wind off the ocean was blowing in heavy, damp gusts. I crossed my arms to stay warm.

The passenger door of the van swung open, and Josh jumped out holding his backpack. He closed the door, slung his backpack over one shoulder, and ran toward me, squinting in the wind. When he got to the top step, where I was standing, he turned and waved to his mom, but she didn't pull away. The van just sat there.

I was about to ask Josh what was going on, when the side door of the van slid open and Jessica poked her head out.

"Jessica?" I said. "What's she doing here?"

"Your mom asked her along," Josh said. "She and Bonnie are going to have a sleepover."

"Oh, *man*," I said. "How could Mom do this to us? They're going to be up all night giggling. How are we supposed to keep watch for a monster when they're doing each other's hair in the next room?"

Jessica climbed out of the van holding a grocery bag crammed full of her stuff.

"She couldn't find her backpack," Josh explained. "It was there one minute and then it was gone."

"How do you think she manages it?"

"I have no idea."

Jessica waved to her mom and jogged across the uneven ground to us, her hair blowing across her face.

At the dinner table it was Bonnie's turn to say grace. Before she bowed her head, she looked at the platter of steaks in the middle of the table, and her own plate of rice and vegetables. She looked us each in the eye before she bowed her head.

"Dear Lord," Bonnie prayed. ' our friends and family and this chance ner together. And thank you, Lord, for this too

There was a short pause, but no *amen* came. I opened one eye to see what was going on. Bonnie still had her head bowed and her palms pressed together under her chin. I closed my eyes again.

"And," Bonnie continued, "thank you for the happy little cow who got killed in the prime of his life and cut up into pieces so *some of the people* at this table could eat him." Another pause. "Amen."

We all opened our eyes. Dad gave Bonnie one of his looks, and I knew that if Josh and Jessica weren't there, she'd be in deep trouble. Mom had a forced smile on her face.

Jessica looked at the platter piled with steaming steaks in the center of the table. "I think I'll just have a baked potato," she said.

Mom glared at Bonnie and then turned, smiling to Jessica. "Oh, come on," she said to Jessica. "Don't let Bonnie bully you. Go ahead and have one if you want." Mom picked up the platter and held it out to her.

Jessica stared at the steaks. She was no doubt imagining Bessie, the happy cow in Bonnie's prayer, frolicking in some green pasture. She shook her head. She looked like she might burst into tears. "I think I'll just have a potato," she said.

"You sure?" Mom said, the smile still fixed on her face. "I made one just for you."

Jessica looked down at her empty plate and shook her head. Mom glared at Bonnie again.

Josh cleared his throat. "It's OK, Mrs. Dolan," he said. "She probably would have just lost it anyway."

Not long after dinner, the storm rolled in. Josh and I sat by the fire and watched television while Bonnie and Jessica sat on either side of the coffee table playing Mancala. Water hammered on the windows facing the bay, and the waves crashed on the boulders below. On top of that, the foghorn blared away out on the cliff. It was hard to hear the television.

A little after 9:00, Mom and Dad went up to bed, and the two girls went up to Bonnie's room—to do each other's hair and giggle, no doubt. Josh and I stayed downstairs alone. We turned off the television and sat in front of the fire watching the flames, waiting for the thunder and lightning to begin. Neither of us said much.

I had been worried that there was a monster when I was at Jeffrey's house in broad daylight, and I'd been nervous again when I was crossing the bay in my skiff on a bright afternoon. But it was nothing compared with the worry I felt now in the middle of a dark, stormy night, way out on Lighthouse Point. I stared silently at the glowing logs in the fireplace and tried not to see faces in them. I knew I'd feel a lot better once the night was over, and we had proved there was no monster.

After a while, the wind picked up. I don't know if all lighthouses are this way, but when there's a big wind blowing in off the ocean, it makes a creepy moaning sound in the tower. It sounds just like a ghost in an old movie, and it started while we sat watching the fire. Believe me, it wasn't a sound I wanted to hear tonight.

Once the thunder and lightning began, we went up to my room, where we'd keep our watch with a pair of Dad's binoculars. As we passed Bonnie's door, we could hear squeals and giggles inside, and I felt a pang of jealousy. I wished I were having such a good time tonight.

As soon as I'd closed the bedroom door behind me, a bright flash lit up the curtained window facing the bay. Both of us jumped. I held my breath and counted. One alligator. Two alligator. Three alligator. When I got to the ninth alligator, a crack of thunder rumbled across the sky. The storm was still pretty far out over the ocean.

I went to the window and pulled back the curtain. All I could see was my reflection. I looked back at Josh. He sat on my bed, looking a little sleepy. "I can't see," I told him. "Turn out the light."

Josh reached over to my bedside lamp and switched it off. I pulled back the curtain again. The wind drove the rain right at the window, so it was just a shimmering, black blur outside. "I can't see a thing," I said. "It's raining too hard."

Josh joined me at the window. We stood there in silence, looking at our own dim reflections. It was pointless. There was no way to see what was going on in the bay from inside the house. "Now what do we do?" I said.

"We're going to have to go up in the tower," Josh said. "We can get outside the glass up there, can't we?"

I let the curtain fall back over the window again. Josh didn't like to admit that he was scared of the water—and the truth was, I didn't like to admit that I was scared of heights. I *hated* going up in the lighthouse tower. Even climbing the spiral staircase gave me the willies.

I swallowed hard. "So in the middle of an electrical storm we're going to climb to the top of a lighthouse?" I said. "Why not just stick our thumbs in a light socket?"

"We'll be OK," Josh promised. "The storm is still way out over the ocean."

"I don't know," I said. "I was kind of hoping we *wouldn't* get struck by lightning tonight."

"Look, if you have a better idea, I'd like to hear it," Josh told me. "It's the only way we'll be able to prove there isn't a monster out there in the bay."

Another flash lit up the window. I counted out loud this time. Seven alligators. The lightning was still pretty far away.

"If it comes any closer, we'll come right back down," Josh promised.

I thought about it a moment. "OK," I said. "But if I get struck by lightning, I'm going to be pretty ticked."

A narrow corridor connected the house with the lighthouse, and as we slipped through it—the rain raking loudly across the roof above our heads—I ransacked my mind for a good excuse for us *not* to go up in the lighthouse tower.

I stopped at the foot of the winding staircase. "You go first," I told Josh. "You're the guest."

Josh gave me a look and started up the spiraling dark stairs. I gripped the stair rail and tried to stay close behind him. In a couple of turns, I was already breathless.

"So how many steps are there?" Josh wanted to know. "Are we almost there, or what?"

"I can't say I've ever counted them," I told him. "But we're not even close to the top."

Although it was pretty dark on the stairs—a single bare lightbulb lit each turn, and a few of the bulbs had burned out—the heat made it easy to know when we were getting near the top. A million-candlepower beacon generates a lot of heat.

We finally climbed up the small ladder to the beacon deck. The huge mirror and lens rotated on their oiled axis, and it was so bright we had to squeeze our eyes shut each time it came around.

When the light is on, it's impossible to see out the glass windows—it's like being trapped in a hall of mirrors—especially during a rainstorm when all the windows are glazed with water. The windows up there are more than an inch thick, so they don't crack from the heat inside and the cold outside.

Josh pushed open the small door below the glass and crawled out on the slippery metal deck Dad uses when he cleans the outside of the glass. The deck is just a steel grid with a tall railing around it—that way it can't get flooded in a rainstorm and short-circuit the light. I looked up through the open doorway at Josh's legs. Even though the roof of the lighthouse sheltered the outer walkway from the rain, the air outside was damp on my face.

If I hated being up in the lighthouse tower, I hated being out on the deck a million times more. It's open to the wind and rain, and you can see through the grid you're standing on to the rocks and the crashing waves far below. There's quite a view from the tower on a clear day, but if you're even a little afraid of heights, it can be terrifying.

I squeezed my eyes shut and offered a silent prayer. When I opened my eyes, Josh was reaching his hand down to me. I flirted with the idea of turning and making a run for it down the winding stairs. But, of course, I couldn't. I'd never hear the end of it. I reached out and clutched Josh's hand. He pulled me up onto the windy steel deck. I gripped the railing with both hands and pulled myself up on wobbly legs.

To the south I could barely make out the blurry lights of town through the downpour, and each time the light came around, all I could see were the sheets of rain it lit up.

"Careful," Josh said. "It's slippery."

I felt a little dizzy, so I turned to face the light. I squeezed my eyes shut and felt the heat of the lamp pass across my face.

"I don't think the monster's actually going to come from that direction," Josh said.

I took a deep breath and turned around. My hand immediately shot out and gripped the railing. Josh stood grinning at me. He wasn't holding the handrail at all. "You're not scared of heights, are you?" he asked.

"I'm just a little tired from the climb," I told him.

I grasped the rail with both hands and forced myself to look out at the stormy bay. The churning sea glimmered as the light swept across it. Any ship unfortunate enough to be out on the sea tonight would see us as two black specks against the light. It occurred to me that we'd also look that way to any sea monster that might be watching at the moment.

"So what are we looking for?" Josh asked, leaning way over the rail.

"I don't know," I said. "A monster, I guess. Or anything out of the usual."

"You're going to have to help me out here," Josh said. "What do you *usually* see up here on a stormy night?"

"You got me," I said. "You think I stand out here in the rain every chance I get?"

Josh looked up at the sky as the beam of light swept across the dark behind us, lighting up the sheets of rain. "How far away is the lightning now?" he asked.

Lightning? What with my fear of heights, I'd completely forgotten about the lightning, but suddenly I felt an electric prickling at the back of my neck. Another fear gripped me. Thank you, Josh Prichard.

"The tower got struck by lightning once when I was a little kid," I said. "It melted two panes of glass and cracked the rest." I looked over at Josh hopefully. "You think it's true what they say?" I asked him, "You know, that it never strikes twice in the same place?"

Josh shrugged. "How would it remember where it struck before?" he said. "It's lightning." That was a good question, and it didn't make me feel any more comfortable.

Josh started moving away from me along the curved railing.

"Hey, where are you going?" I said, gripping the rail and following him.

"I want to see if I can see the inn from up here," he said.

"We're supposed to be watching for the monster," I told him.

Josh kept moving. "Maybe he's heading over to my house," he said. "Too bad Jessica's *here*."

He stopped and looked out at the lights of town across the cove, finally taking hold of the rail. "There's the pier," he said, leaning forward and peering into the rain. "And there's the grocery store." I arrived next to him. I gripped the rail with both hands. My knees shook under me. The light came around, and for a few seconds the town disappeared behind a bright curtain of rain.

"And there's some kind of monster," Josh said matter-of-factly when the light swept past.

I thought he was joking, but then I noticed a dark, shapeless mass moving through the water of the cove. It didn't have the sharply defined shape of a boat, but it was too solid to be a school of fish. It was about a hundred yards out on the water, slipping silently toward us.

"What *is* that?" Josh asked.

The light crept around in its oiled socket, and as its beam swept across the surface of the water again, it lit up what looked like a giant white tentacle, which immediately slipped beneath the churning water. The scene disappeared again behind the glare of the light.

When the light moved on, the shape had disappeared. Empty water stretched before us to the bleary lights of Boulder Bay. The thing, whatever it was, had vanished.

We stood there in stunned amazement for a few seconds, both of us gripping the railing. I didn't know what to say. The whole point of this vigil was to prove to ourselves that there *wasn't* a monster. This had put a crimp in that plan.

I looked down below us. The waves crashed and foamed around the boulders. It was a long way down. A flash of lightning, far out to sea, lit up the glistening rocks like a photograph. I half expected to see the Creature of Terror Cove sliding its huge rubbery body out of the waves to begin its quivering climb up the tower toward us.

"What do you say we head downstairs?" I said softly, my heart pounding in my chest.

"I was about to suggest the same thing," Josh said.

I was the first to scramble through the doorway, and the two of us sprinted down the dizzying coil of stairs, through the corridor, and into the safety of the house.

When I was safe on the top bunk, the storm came ashore in earnest, howling and crashing and moaning in the lighthouse tower. I lay awake, my eyes squeezed shut, the covers pulled up to my nose, while Josh snored below me on the lower bunk.

I don't mind admitting it: I was scared. I prayed that God would protect us, and I thought of Daniel in the Bible. Was he scared all night in the lions' den, or did he just lie down and go to sleep, using one of the cubs as a pillow? I thought about it for a while. I liked the idea that maybe he was scared too—just like me—even though he was a Bible guy. And I knew that the same God who protected him could protect me too.

As dawn broke, the storm began to let up, and I managed to fall asleep with the rain hissing on the peaked roof above me.

Chapter 5

When I woke up, the sky was still drizzling, and Josh still snored on the bunk below me. I dragged myself out of bed and trudged over to the window. I pulled back the curtain and peeked outside. The storm had passed. Water dripped from the eaves, and the grass down below looked tousled and slick with water. The ocean was choppy in the wind, and beyond, at the other end of the cove, smoke rose from the chimneys in town. It was hard to make out much more through the rain-dotted glass. I'd have to go outside for a better look.

I went over and looked at Josh. He coughed and grumbled and rolled over on the bunk, his hair as spiked and disorderly as the windswept grass below my window. I thought I'd let him sleep.

I quietly pulled on the same clothes I'd worn the day before and slipped downstairs without waking Josh. Bonnie and Jessica sat at the kitchen table eating cereal.

"About time you got up," Bonnie said.

I glanced at the clock on the microwave oven. It was only 6:30.

"Where are Mom and Dad?" I asked her.

"They headed to the Coast Guard station for cleaning supplies," she told me. "The door up in the tower blew open somehow during the storm, and the whole place is a mess. Don't expect to see them until lunch time."

I felt myself blush. The door was open? I tried to remember if we'd closed it last night when we'd come sprinting down the stairs, but most of last night was an anxious blur.

"So what are you guys going to do today?" Bonnie asked. She sounded as if she might want to tag along.

"I thought we'd go fishing," I said, knowing she wouldn't want any part of it. "Want to come along?"

Jessica's eyes lit up. She leaned forward. She was about to say something when Bonnie cut her off. "That's *horrible*," Bonnie squealed. "How would you like it if a big fish hooked you through the lip and dragged you through the water? It's barbaric. I hope you fall in the water and get eaten by sharks."

"Fine," I said. "Then *don't* come along."

"Fine," Bonnie said.

Jessica looked disappointed. She leaned back in her chair again. "So what are *we* going to do?" she asked Bonnie.

"Maybe we'll go check out the tide pools and make sure everything's OK after the storm," Bonnie told her.

It was just like her. She'd happily feed her brother to man-eating sharks and then go down to the tide pools to make sure the sea snails were comfortable.

"That sounds like a riotous good time," I said. "Nothing like frolicking with hermit crabs and sea urchins. You know those urchins make great omelettes."

Bonnie stood up from the table. "Come on, Jessica," she said. "Let's get out of here." She strode past me and took her jacket from the hook by the kitchen door. "I don't want to be in the same kitchen with this barbarian," she said, pulling her jacket on.

Jessica pushed back her chair and stood up. She obviously wasn't terribly excited about spending her day with sea snails and mussels. She shuffled over to the kitchen door where Bonnie was waiting for her and looked up at the empty coat hook. "Hey, where's my jacket?" she said. "It was hanging here a minute ago."

Once Bonnie and Jessica had disappeared over the hill to the north of the lighthouse, I went outside and stood in the wind, looking out over the bay to the south. Except for a single sailboat, the waters of the bay were empty. No monster. No mysterious shapes. Nothing out of the ordinary.

I was standing there for more than a minute when I realized that the sailboat was making no headway on the choppy water of the bay. I watched it awhile. It floated to and fro, obviously not anchored. I couldn't see anyone on deck.

I ran to the kitchen and got Dad's binoculars. I raced outside on the slick wet grass and turned the binoculars on the sailboat. The deck was empty, and no lights were on in the cabin. The stern of the boat swung around in the wind, and I saw that the cabin door was wide open. If there was anyone on board, they weren't paying much attention. If the boat drifted any closer to the rocks, it would be dashed to pieces pretty quickly.

I ran inside to the phone. I picked up the receiver, but it was dead. It didn't take much to knock out the phone line on Lighthouse Point, and the storm had done it again. Dad's Coast Guard radio would still work, but he was gone, and I didn't know how to operate it.

I ran up the stairs to where Josh was still a snoring heap on the lower bunk. I shook him. He yelled and started swinging at me with both fists. I jumped back. "Whoa, Josh," I said. "Relax. It's just me."

Josh sat bolt upright and looked around at the room, as if trying to remember how he got here. His hair was standing up on one side. He rubbed his eyes. "Man," he said excitedly. "I was having a terrible dream. We were out on your boat."

"Skiff," I told him. "But—"

"And the monster dragged you overboard," he went on, talking so fast I could barely keep up with him. "And then it came after me, except I was on a bicycle then."

"But there's—"

"And I was in the auditorium at school, riding up and down the aisles. And then the monster was Mrs. Evans, my third grade teacher, and she—"

I clapped my hand over his mouth. "Would you shut up about the stupid dream a minute?" I interrupted. "We've got to do something. There's a boat loose on the bay. It's going to get wrecked against the rocks. There might be people on board."

I took my hand off his mouth. "Huh?" he said.

"There's no time to lose," I told him. I grabbed him by the arm and dragged him off the bunk onto the floor. "Get dressed!" I shouted. "Hurry!"

Josh pulled a sweatshirt over his head. It was inside out, but what did that matter? I pulled on my jacket while he tied his shoes.

"Come on!" I shouted. I burst out into the hallway and dashed down the stairs. I could hear Josh stumbling behind me, still not fully awake.

Josh stood on the lighthouse dock looking down at me. He wouldn't budge. "Just shut up and get in the boat," I told him.

"Skiff," he corrected me. "And what do I need to go along for?"

"It's going to take two of us to rescue the boat," I told him. The skiff rocked gently beneath my feet. "You're going to have to stay on the skiff while I climb up and anchor the sailboat. There's no other way."

"I hate boats," he said.

"I know," I told him. "But get over it. Someone's life may be in danger."

Josh sighed. He stepped down into the skiff. He crawled on his hands and knees to the seat at the bow end and sat on it. "I'd rather be chased through the auditorium by Mrs. Evans than ride in your stupid boat," he complained. He opened the locker at the front of the skiff and grabbed the bright orange life vest.

"What's this?" he said. He pulled out the flare gun Pete had given me years ago when he'd bought a new one.

"It's a flare gun," I said. "Don't play with it."

"What's it for?"

"It's a distress signal," I said. "Put it back."

He looked down at the flare gun in his hand. "I'm *feeling* pretty distressed," he said. "I think I'll hang on to it."

"Fine," I said. "Just sit down so we can go."

Josh managed to pull the life vest over his head without letting go of the flare gun. He pulled the straps tight and clutched the seat beneath him with both hands, the flare gun balanced across his knees.

I shook my head and bent down to pull the cord that starts the engine.

"Whoa," Josh said, clutching his seat tighter. "Sit down. You're making the boat rock."

I started the engine. "We're not going anywhere until you untie us," I told Josh. He looked over at the dock and down at the water. Without standing, he leaned way over and pulled our line off the cleat.

Josh sat in the bow as we puttered across the choppy water toward the sailboat. I watched him huddled there, squinting in the wind, pulling the life jacket tightly around him. He kept muttering to himself, but I couldn't hear him over the drone of the engine. The swells on the bay were pretty big, and as we headed into the deep water, Josh's face grew more and more pale.

"You know what my favorite Bible story is?" I asked him. He didn't answer. "It's the one about Daniel in the lions' den," I said. "If God could deliver Daniel from a bunch of hungry lions, He can protect us from some choppy water."

Josh shrugged. "*My* favorite Bible story is about a wall that falls down," he said. "It looked really sturdy, but it still fell down all the same. How old is this boat, anyway?"

I just shook my head. There was no talking to him. The two of us chugged through the water in silence.

"I don't recognize the boat," I said when we got closer. "Does it belong to anyone in town?"

Josh twisted to look behind him in the direction of the boat. "You got me," he said. "I'm a landlubber. Boats are your department."

Out on the open bay, the water was a lot rougher than it looked from high up on Lighthouse Point. Whitecapped waves cut across the bow like shark's teeth, and the wind kept blowing us toward the land. It was surprising that the sailboat wasn't already dashed to pieces on the rocks.

Josh saw me struggle to keep the skiff on course.

"You sure this is a good idea?" he said. "Maybe I should shoot the flare gun."

"We're fine," I told him. "I know what I'm doing." But in truth I was a little nervous. A little skiff like mine wasn't made to be out on a day like this.

When we got close to the sailboat, it was clearly untethered, and it bucked up and down on the waves. It would be hard to get close to it in this weather without banging into it. "Maybe we should go for help," Josh said reasonably. "You know what this reminds me of?"

I knew exactly what it reminded him of—the empty sailboat in *Terror Cove*. I'd been thinking the same thing, but I kept my mouth shut.

"This is just like in the movie," he said. "That couple who got eaten off their boat. It's just like that. Maybe I should shoot the flare gun."

I held my tongue and tried to find a safe approach. The big sailboat tilted and dove on the waves. No lights were on inside, and the cabin door swung to and fro each time a swell passed under it.

"Look, we can see there's no one on board," Josh insisted. "Isn't that what we came to see? Isn't that enough?"

"There's nothing to worry about," I told him. "You're not scared, are you?"

Josh didn't answer. I steered the skiff around to the stern of the sailboat. A chrome ladder ran down the back and almost touched the white-capped waves.

"If I can get us close enough, I'll climb on board," I said. "Maybe I can drop the anchor."

"I'm not sure I like this plan," Josh said. "How come I have to stay on this thing alone?"

I glared at him. "OK then," I said. "*You* climb aboard the sailboat."

He looked at the bucking sailboat, its mast swinging back and forth like the metronome on Mom's piano. "You know, I'm not crazy about either alternative," he said.

"Look," I told him. "I'll tie the skiff to the ladder so you won't drift away."

"What kind of knot?" he wanted to know.

"What do you *mean,* what kind of knot?" I said. "You don't know anything about knots." I sighed in exasperation. "Which knot would you like me to tie?"

Josh thought a moment. "One of the better ones," he told me.

"OK," I said. "I'll tie one of the better ones."

I steered the skiff toward the stern of the sailboat. It was rough going, and I had to circle around twice to get a good approach. I held the line to the skiff with one hand and steered with the other. When I got close enough to the sailboat, I cut the engine and grabbed the chrome ladder with the hand that held the line.

The stern of the sailboat rose up suddenly and nearly yanked me out of the skiff. I climbed up on the ladder and tied the skiff securely. I looked down at Josh from the ladder. He didn't seem too pleased to be alone in a skiff on rough water. "Use the oar to keep from bumping the sailboat," I told him.

Josh didn't move a muscle. He just sat there looking pale and worried.

"That way the skiff won't get smashed to pieces and sink," I told him.

Josh grabbed the oar from the bottom of the boat and began poking the sailboat, like you'd poke a dead skunk with a stick. He kept the flare gun nearby.

I climbed onto the rolling deck. I wasn't sure what I was going to do. I had no plan really. As I was climbing the ladder, I'd flirted with the idea of sailing the boat back to the marina, but one look at it and I knew I was out of my league. It looked much bigger, now that I was actually aboard.

It was a beautiful sailboat, with every kind of fancy thing you can imagine—it must have cost a mint—and yet here it was, abandoned and adrift in a bay, surrounded by rocks and boulders. The wind raked across the deck, and the fine ocean spray blew directly into my face.

It was hard to keep my footing on the moving deck, but I made my way to the bow and released the anchor. It splashed into the water and dragged the chain after it. In a few seconds, I felt the difference. The sailboat drifted leeward and tugged on the chain.

I went to the open cabin door and looked inside. It was a beautiful setup, but the place was a mess. There was a little galley and a table, a television, and a stereo. The deck was slick with water, and papers and books were strewn all over the place. On the table was a plate with half a bagel on it. The other half of the bagel was wedged in a corner of the floor along with a broken coffee mug. It looked as if someone had been interrupted while eating.

An image from *Terror Cove* flickered into my mind—a rubbery tentacle slipping out of the waves and up onto the deck of the sailboat—but I tried to shrug it off.

At the far end of the cabin was a door. I tried it, but it was locked. I knocked with the side of my fist. "Hello?" I called through the door. "Anyone on board?" There was no answer.

I was turning to leave when I saw the radio. I switched on the power and the display lit up. I went back out on the deck and back to the stern. Josh, looking bloodless and cold, was still poking at the stern of the sailboat with his oar. "About time," he said when he saw me.

"Climb on up," I told him. "It's safer up here. We can call for help on the radio. They'll take us in to the marina."

"I'm not sure I want to go up there," Josh told me.

"There's nothing up here," I assured him. "The boat is empty." I thought of the locked door in the cabin. "Come on up."

"You're sure the monster isn't there?"

"The giant, glowing pterodactyl octopus?" I asked. "Can't say I saw one."

Josh didn't look happy, even though the wind was letting up. He pulled on the line I'd tied to the ladder until the skiff was next to the sailboat. He glanced around him at the waves and got a good grip on the ladder.

"It'll be easier to climb the ladder if you leave the flare gun behind," I told him.

Josh reluctantly set down the flare gun. He pulled himself out of the skiff and shakily climbed the ladder.

As soon as we were on solid ground again, Josh just wanted to go home. We stood on the public dock at the marina while Officer Borders supervised the dock workers who were tying up the sailboat. He'd taken down all the particulars about the boat so they could find out who owned it. I watched him jotting in his little notebook. He was far enough away that Josh and I could talk without him hearing.

"Shouldn't we tell him?" I asked. "Shouldn't we let him know what's going on?"

Josh still looked pale. "I just want to go home," he told me. "I don't feel so good."

"We can't just walk away from this," I insisted. "We've got to tell someone. Jeffrey's family is gone. Whoever was fishing at the end of this dock is gone. Now the people who were sailing this boat are gone too." I lowered my voice. "There's something out in that bay, and we're the only ones who know what's going on." Just saying those words gave me the willies. I glanced out at the bay and back at Josh.

Josh stepped closer to me. "So what are we going to tell him?" he whispered. "We saw a dumb monster movie and now we think it's coming true? You think he's going to believe that?"

"But we've got evidence," I told him. "And we saw it with our own eyes."

"Evidence?" Josh said. "What evidence do we have? We saw something in the middle of a rainstorm, from the top of a lighthouse. You think *that* will convince him? You think he's going to take our word for it?"

I knew it all sounded crazy, but what if it was true? We couldn't just go away and forget about it. *"Lives may be in danger!"* I told Josh—a little too loudly. Officer Borders immediately turned to look at me. I clapped a hand over my mouth.

"Lives in danger?" Officer Borders asked. He tucked his notebook into his shirt pocket and walked over to where we were standing. "What are you boys talking about?"

I looked at Josh and then at the sailboat tied up beside us and then out at the choppy water of the bay. I knew Josh was right. If I told Officer Borders, he'd just laugh, and he'd probably go back to the station and tell his mom about the two stupid kids who thought they were in a monster movie. What proof *did* we have? An empty boat. Some abandoned fishing gear. A broken window at Jeffrey's house. Officer Borders hadn't seen what we saw. We'd never convince him.

Once we were safely back in Josh's room at the inn, the color came back to his face. He began to relax, but there was still a lot on both our minds.

"We've got to get help," I said, pacing up and down on Josh's floor while he lay on the bed staring at the ceiling. "But who do you call in a situation like this?"

"Maybe we could call that professor guy in the movie," Josh said. He swung his feet over the edge of his bed and sat up. "The one at the university. The one with that reverse-proton-ray-gun-thingy."

I stopped pacing and glared at him. "The professor?" I inquired. "The professor who had an office in the grocery store? That's who you want to call?"

Josh shrugged sheepishly. "I don't know," he said. "Everything *else* in the movie seems to be happening."

"Yeah, OK," I said. "We'll go into town and see if there's a university there we've never noticed before. That sounds like a brilliant plan to me."

"Look, if you have a better idea, I'd sure like to hear it," Josh told me.

"I don't think anyone could come up with a *worse* idea," I told him. "That's about the third stupidest thing I've heard in my life. And the other two were *also* your ideas."

"It's not such a bad idea," Josh said. "All we have to do is find some professor *somewhere* who has a reverse proton beam. Maybe we could borrow it."

"It was just a prop in a dumb movie," I reminded him.

"Yeah, and the monster was just some kind of puppet in the movie," he said. "But that didn't keep it from eating about a dozen people in the last few days. Maybe the ray gun really exists too."

I sighed. "OK," I said. "Let's say the stupid ray guns exist—how in the world are we going to find one?"

Josh sat there a moment thinking. "Maybe we could buy one on eBay," Josh said. "That's where my dad got his golf clubs."

I stood a moment looking down at him, blinking and speechless. I shook my head. "We now have a new first place leader in the stupid idea standings," I announced.

"It's not *that* stupid," Josh said. "Maybe we could find one on the Internet—everything in the world is on the Internet."

Josh rolled off the bed and pulled out the chair in front of his desk. In a couple of minutes he'd logged onto the Internet and typed "reverse proton" into a search engine. He clicked his mouse.

"There," he said. "If there's a reverse proton ray gun anywhere in the world, we're about to find it."

To my amazement, the computer came up with something. Josh clicked on the address, and in a few seconds we were at a Web site called "Vancepro Films."

"What is this?" Josh asked. "I thought we'd end up somewhere scientific."

"Scroll down," I told him, reading over his shoulder. "I think this is about movies." Line after line rose to the top of the screen and disappeared.

"Hold on," Josh said. "Look at this." He moved the cursor to highlight the words *Terror Cove.*

"It's about the movie," I said.

There were titles of dozens of other movies like *Return of Iguana Man* and *Invasion from Planet X.*

"It must be the Web page for the movie studio," Josh said. "It's not really about ray guns."

"A lot of help this does," I said. "We've already *seen* the movie."

"But it might be just what we need," Josh said. "Maybe we can E-mail the guy who made the movie. He's the guy who invented this monster. Maybe *he'll* know where we can get one of those guns."

"I don't know," I said. "He's a movie director, not a scientist."

"It's worth a try isn't it?" Josh said. "What harm can it do to send him an E-mail?"

Dear Mr. Vance—

You don't know us. We're just a couple of kids who live in Boulder Bay, which is where you once filmed the movie *Terror Cove.* Well, we both saw the movie last week, and now everything that happened in the movie seems to be happening in real life, which is kind of weird. And since one of us lives in the lighthouse, we're getting kind of nervous.

We were just wondering if you could tell us where we could get a reverse proton ray gun, like the one the professor in the movie had. If you'll just let us know where we can get one, we won't bother you any more.

Sincerely,
Josh Prichard and Danny Dolan

Chapter 6

D anny," Mom called up the stairs to me. "It's for you. It's Josh. I'll leave the phone on the counter."

I ran down the stairs to the kitchen and picked up the phone off the counter. Through the window I could see Mom working outside in one of her flowerbeds. I put the phone to my ear. "What's up?"

"He's here," Josh whispered into the phone, like he didn't want to be overheard.

"Who's where?" I whispered back, even though I was alone in the kitchen and no one could possibly hear me.

"Vic Vance," Josh told me. "He just showed up at the inn. He wants a room."

"Vic Vance?" I said. "Who's that?"

"He's the guy who made *Terror Cove*," Josh said. "He just walked in and asked for a room, and then he said something about going up to the lighthouse because of the monster. He's real loud, and we've got some other guests here this week. It's kind of embarrassing."

"Did you tell him who you are?" I asked. "Did you tell him *we* sent him the E-mail?"

"No way," Josh said. "I don't want anyone to know. He's too embarrassing. He keeps stopping people and asking them if they've seen a monster. He keeps going around *looking* at everything."

"What's wrong with looking at things?"

"He's not doing it like a normal person," Josh said. "He keeps holding his hands up like a frame and looking through them. He keeps grabbing my chin and twisting it around so he can see my profile. It's embarrassing."

"Relax," I told Josh. "Nobody knows who he is."

"Are you kidding?" Josh said. "He keeps giving people his card. He's only been here ten minutes and I have four of them."

"What's his card say?" I heard a rustling on the other end of the line.

"It says 'Vic Vance, Director,'" Josh said. "And then the phone number's crossed out and a new one's written in red felt pen. We've got to get rid of him."

"But maybe he can help us."

"I don't know, Danny. He seems kind of nutty. Why don't I just send him over to the lighthouse, and then maybe he'll go home."

"No way," I said. "Don't send him over here."

"Well, what do I do?" he asked. "He came here to see us, but I don't want to be seen with him."

I tied my skiff up to the public dock and practically sprinted to Josh's family inn. When I came in the front door, Josh was behind the counter. He looked like he was wound pretty tight.

"Thank goodness you're here," Josh said. "He checked in. He took his suitcase up to his room, but he said he'd be right down. He said he had pressing business to attend to. He said he'd probably be in town a week or so, until he'd made it safe for humanity. He's going to make us look like idiots. What are we going to do?"

"Relax," I told Josh. "He couldn't be that bad. We can handle him."

Josh just sighed and shook his head. "Come on, Danny," he said. "Let me introduce you."

All through the second-floor hallway we could hear him singing—a booming baritone that made the floor vibrate. One of the other guests opened her door and peeked out, but closed it again when she saw us coming along the hallway. We paused outside Mr. Vance's door. I looked at Josh and then knocked.

The singing stopped abruptly. "Come in," a voice inside bellowed.

I twisted the knob and pushed the door open. I stood back politely so Josh could enter first, but he pushed me in ahead of him.

Vic Vance's back was turned to me. He was looking out the window and down at Clark Street. He was a huge mountain of a man—at least six and a half feet tall—and he was wearing a loud suit with a checkered pattern. His black hair was curly in back.

Then he turned to look at me.

"Stop!" he shouted suddenly. I froze. My heart began to race. He held his hand up like Officer Borders does when he's directing traffic. "Stop right there!"

I felt myself begin to shake.

"Turn slowly and look at the window," he told me. I did what he said. "Now look back this way."

I looked back at him. He was now holding his hands in front of his face. He made a rectangle of his index fingers and thumbs and peered through it at me. This must have been what Josh was talking about.

"Great lighting," he said. "Absolutely perfect." He went back to the window and looked out again. I wasn't sure if I was still supposed to freeze. I glanced behind me at Josh. He shrugged.

"Mr. Vance?" I said nervously. "I'm Danny Dolan. This is Josh Prichard. He's the one who sent you the E-mail."

Josh punched me on the shoulder from behind. "We *both* sent you the E-mail," he corrected me.

Mr. Vance turned slowly from the window and sized up the two of us. I had the impulse to back toward the door, but Josh was more or less hiding behind me, and there was nowhere to go.

Mr. Vance just stared down at us a few seconds, looking us over. His hand suddenly shot out toward me, and I stepped back onto Josh's foot. Mr. Vance grabbed me by the chin with his beefy hand and twisted my head this way and that, while Josh hopped around behind me groaning and holding his foot. "You've got the look," the huge man told me.

"Thank you," I told Vic Vance. "Thank you very much." I didn't know what else to say.

It was Josh's idea that we all go to the Deep End Diner for lunch. He said he'd buy. I knew he just wanted to get Vic Vance out of the hotel to some place more anonymous. The Deep End Diner was a dimly lit, out-of-the-way place that had few customers until the dinner hour. No one would really notice Mr. Vance if we took him there. And who knew? We might be able to get rid of him pretty quick. Maybe he could tell us where to get a reverse proton beam, and he'd be out of town before sundown.

"Great idea, son," Mr. Vance said. "We'll do lunch. I'll go bring the car around front." He tousled Josh's hair and strode to the door. The windows rattled with each heavy step he took.

When his footsteps faded down the hallway, I heaved a sigh of relief.

"What are we going to do?" Josh said. "I'm not sure which I'd rather have in town—that guy or the monster."

"It'll be OK," I promised. "We'll get him to tell us about the reverse proton beam and send him on his merry way. No one will even know he was in town."

But any hope we had of keeping Mr. Vance undercover was blown when we stepped outside the inn and found him parked at the curb in a red

Cadillac convertible the size of an aircraft carrier. When he saw us at the top of the steps, he honked his horn—as if we might not have noticed him. But of course his car didn't just honk, it played a loud stanza of "There's No Business Like Show Business." Curtains up and down the street were drawn back to see who was playing such an obnoxious tune.

I beat Josh down the steps and touched the Cadillac. "You get shotgun," I told Josh. He glared at me and pulled open the huge door.

"Now, what's this about *Terror Cove?*" Mr. Vance said. He slapped the tabletop with his palm, and the ice in our water glasses jingled.

I looked from our booth at the rest of the restaurant. It was just a reflex—no one else was in the diner. "It's really nothing, sir," I said. "We just need to borrow the reverse proton beam you used in the movie."

"Come again?" He leaned his huge moon of a face over the table at me. I squirmed in my seat. I looked at Josh, who was sitting beside me, for help.

"In the movie," Josh explained. "You know, at the end of *Terror Cove* when the monster attacks the lighthouse, and the professor shoots him with that ray-gun thingy? That's what we need."

91

"Ah, yes," Mr. Vance said, leaning back in his seat, a proud smile spreading across his face. "I know what you mean. The reverse proton beam. That was quite an ending."

"Do you still have it?" I asked.

"Have what?"

"The reverse proton beam," I said. "We need it to kill the monster."

"No, of course not," he said. "That was just a bunch of old vacuum cleaner parts glued together and spray painted silver." He leaned in and lowered his voice confidentially. "It was a movie," he said, as though that might be news to us.

Josh moved his water glass out of the way and leaned forward. "Yeah, but we've got a *real* monster here," he said. "We've seen it with our own eyes. It's eaten about a dozen people already. Since everything else in the movie is coming true, we thought there might really be some kind of monster-killing ray beam thing somewhere."

Mr. Vance grinned across the table at us. "No, boys, the movie wasn't real," he said. He leaned back in his seat and set his hands, palms down, on the table. "It's all just pretend."

Did he think we were idiots? "Yeah," I said. "We know it was just pretend, but it's all coming true."

"True?" he said.

I looked at Josh. "He doesn't get it," I said. "We're going to have to tell him the whole story."

And we did—about Jeffrey, the fishing gear, and the empty boat. We told him what we'd seen from the lighthouse tower during the storm. Mr. Vance just kept rubbing his big jowly chin. "It's all just like in the movie," I said, when we'd finished our story. "And I live in the lighthouse where the monster attacks at the end, so I'm a little concerned."

Mr. Vance folded his hands on the tabletop. "So what do you want from me?"

"Well, since it's *your* monster," Josh said, "we were hoping you could tell us how to get rid of it."

Mr. Vance glanced around. "I don't think it's my monster," he said, suddenly nervous. "It must be someone else's."

"Someone *else's* monster?" I said.

"I'm not responsible," Mr. Vance went on, pointing a beefy finger at the ceiling. "Everyone signed waivers. You'll never prove anything."

"We're not taking you to court," Josh said. "We just thought that maybe you could help. We didn't know who else to ask."

"This isn't going to court?" Mr. Vance looked at us skeptically.

We both shook our heads.

"You'll sign waivers?"

"I don't know what a waiver is," Josh admitted. "But if you'll help us get rid of your monster, I'll sign anything."

Mr. Vance sat back in his chair again. He grew visibly relaxed now that he knew we'd sign waivers. He tapped a thick finger on the tabletop, deep in thought.

I looked at Josh and smiled. We were making progress. Mr. Vance would tell us what to do. He'd bail us out.

"So what did you guys think?" Victor Vance asked suddenly.

I was confused. "About what?" I said.

"Terror Cove," he said. "Some ending, huh? I think next to *Snailzilla* that was my best explosion." He just sat there nodding and grinning to himself.

"Mr. Vance," I said. "Do you think you can help us get rid of the monster or not?"

"Sure thing," he said, snapping his attention back to the table. "Absolutely. I'm great at endings. I must have killed a hundred monsters in my films. And call me Victor."

I glanced over at Josh again. He looked as worried as I felt. Mr. Vance—Victor—might not be as helpful as I'd hoped he'd be. In fact, to be blunt, he *did* seem to be some kind of nut.

"So," I said. "What's *one* way to kill a monster?"

"Well," he said. "In *Snailzilla,* they followed the trail of giant snail dots, and then dropped five tons of salt on him from a helicopter. Talk about an explosion. We used six hundred pounds of real escargot. My ears were ringing for a week after that one." He chuckled. "I kept answering the phone when no one was calling."

I ran my hand down my face.

"But you see, Mr. Vance," Josh said, trying his best to be polite. "This monster lives in *the ocean.* I don't think salt is going to bother him any."

Mr. Vance nodded thoughtfully. "Now that's good thinking, son," he said. "And call me Victor."

Between sips of coffee, Mr. Vance went on to outline other ways he had killed monsters in his movies. A huge mutant rabbit was lured to giant papier-mâché carrots filled with dynamite. A huge Bug Zapper was suspended between the twin towers of the World Trade Center to destroy the giant radioactive moth that had been terrorizing New York City. And Lobsterman had fallen into a big vat of boiling water. Each ended in an explosion for some reason, and none of them seemed very practical to me.

"I'm not sure you appreciate the situation here," I told Mr. Vance. "We're just a couple of kids. We don't have access to explosives or helicopters. Do you have any monster-killing techniques that don't require a lot of overhead?"

"Low budget, huh?"

I slipped my hand into my pocket and jingled my spare change. "Lower than you can imagine," I told him.

"Hmmm," he said. He tapped his fingers on the tabletop. "You're absolutely sure this is my monster?"

"Who else's monster would it be?" Josh asked. It seemed like a reasonable question.

"I don't know," Mr. Vance said. "But there are copyright issues. I can't just go around blowing up any old monster you come across. What if it belongs to some other director? I'm going to have to make a positive I.D. before we go any further."

I looked at Josh. The expression on his face told me he was thinking what I was thinking: that Vic Vance was moonstruck, nutty, unhinged, wacko—pixilated, even. But I could tell Josh and I were both thinking something else as well: this nut was the only adult in the world who would actually believe us. He was our only hope. I sighed.

"So you want to *see* the monster before you'll help us kill it?" I asked.

"Just to be on the safe side," Mr. Vance said.

"And how do you propose we do that?" Josh wanted to know.

"Well, in the script for *Terror Cove,* I made it so the monster only comes out when there's a storm," Mr. Vance said. "When is the next storm coming?"

I looked out the window at the ocean. The sky was steel gray, and a line of black clouds were gathering at the horizon. I swallowed hard. "Just after dark tonight," I said. "There's a new squall line coming in."

Mr. Vance leaned across the table and nodded gravely. "And do we have access to a boat?" he asked us.

"It's a skiff," Josh corrected him.

When I called Mom and told her that I'd be spending the night at Josh's house, she didn't even hesitate to say yes. I'd been secretly hoping she'd pry a little. I was hoping she'd ask a few questions—that she'd get out of me that we planned to go out on the bay in the middle of the rainstorm in my little skiff under the dubious supervision of a lunatic named Vic Vance. I sort of hoped she'd put a quick end to the plan. But she didn't ask.

That night after midnight I was still lying awake on the upper bunk. I hadn't gotten a wink of sleep, and the rain was coming down hard. I looked over at the glowing numbers of Josh's alarm clock. It was nearly 1:00 A.M. Thunder rumbled across the sky and lightning flickered behind the drawn curtains.

Mr. Vance had said he'd come by Josh's room at midnight and knock on the door. It was looking like he'd fallen asleep, and I wasn't about to go wake him up. Spending the night safe and dry in Josh's room was fine with me. When the glowing numbers changed to 1:00, I began to relax. We'd be going nowhere tonight. Maybe I could even get some sleep. I rolled over and faced the wall, smiling.

And then it came: three sharp raps on the door. I froze. I held my breath and pretended to be asleep. The next knock came a little louder. I quietly sat up and listened for Josh stirring on the upper bunk. There wasn't a sound. Josh could sleep through a hurricane.

I looked at the door. The knob twisted this way and that. I'd locked it before I'd climbed into bed. I held still and stayed quiet. Mr. Vance would soon give up and go back to bed. In the crack of light beneath the door, I could see his shadow. He was just parked there, no doubt wondering what he should do.

"Hey, boys," he bellowed, so loud it made the windows in the room vibrate. *"It's time to get up!"*

"Shhhhhhh," I hissed. "You'll wake everybody up."

In half an hour, the three of us were in the skiff, bundled up in our rain gear, chugging away from the dock toward the deep waters of the bay. Mr. Vance sat in the very prow of the ship with his back to us, so Josh was with me at the back to balance things out a little. Mr. Vance looked so huge up there, I was a little surprised that the motor's propeller was still in the water.

The water was choppy and the wind tore in from the ocean, so the rain was hard and slanted. With the wind buffeting us, it was hard to keep the skiff headed straight, but I used the glimmering beacon of the lighthouse as a reference point.

"A little farther," Mr. Vance said, as though he was referring to some kind of map. "And a little to the left."

"It's called port," I called up to him. "And what makes you think that's where the monster will be?"

"It's the perfect shot," he explained. "With the lighthouse in the background, the composition is just right."

I shook my head and aimed us a little to port. We were out on a skiff in the middle of a rainstorm, and Mr. Vance thought he could direct what would happen. Had we lost our minds? What were we doing out here with this crazy lunatic?

Josh was huddled up beside me, silent and shaking. His lips were moving in silent prayer. I felt bad for him. He really hated boating.

"Everything's under control," I told him. "Everything's going to be OK." But as the skiff rose and fell on each passing swell, I honestly wasn't so sure.

"OK," Mr. Vance said suddenly. "This is the spot." He looked out at the bay in front of us, framed by his two hands. "Do you have a parking brake or something?"

"It's called an anchor," I said. "I'm not sure if the line is long enough for this deep in the bay."

"Well, this is where we need to park," he said. "So give it a try."

I let the engine idle and scrambled to the middle of the skiff. I picked up the heavy anchor, which was hooked over the gunwale, and made sure I was clear of the coiled chain. I dangled the anchor over the side and let it drop.

The chain tore down through the water. I watched as coil after coil disappeared over the side. Finally the line went slack. The anchor was resting on the bottom—and I still had a few yards of chain left. I secured the chain. We were parked.

I looked at Mr. Vance. He still sat—a huge hulk—in the bow of the boat, patiently looking out over the water. "So what do we do now?" I asked him.

"We wait," he said. "It should be along any minute."

I went back and sat beside Josh. I turned off the engine. I was getting a little angry at Mr. Vance.

"'It should be along any minute,'" I mimicked. "Where does he get this stuff?"

Josh turned his pale face toward me. "It *is* his monster," he said.

"Oh, don't *you* start going crazy on me," I said. "One nut in the skiff is more than enough." I glanced up at Mr. Vance. "Both of us have to stay sharp tonight," I whispered to Josh. "We're really going to have to keep an eye on this guy. You and I are in the same boat."

"It's a *skiff,*" Josh said.

"It was just a figure of speech," I told him hotly. "And I'll thank *you* to—"

"Yes, boys," Mr. Vance boomed from where he sat at the bow. "That's my monster."

I looked up at where he was sitting, just as the light from the lighthouse swept across the water. About twenty yards from the front of the boat, a giant tentacle rose a couple of yards out of the water. It was gray and dripping with water.

I stood up. It was a reflex.

The light passed, and the tentacle slipped beneath the surface again. I just stood there blinking. The skiff rocked beneath my feet. For a few seconds everything was eerily silent, except for the falling of the rain.

"Let's go home," Josh suggested.

"I'm in complete agreement," I said. I grabbed the rope that starts the engine and gave it a yank. "Go pull up the anchor," I told Josh.

"*I'm* not going up there," Josh said.

"Look, if you want to get out of here, we're going to need to pull up the anchor," I told him. "Get a move on. There's a monster out there."

Josh sighed and crawled to the middle of the skiff. I put the engine in reverse and we drifted backwards and tugged on the anchor. "Come on," I yelled. "Get it off the bottom."

Josh clearly didn't want to reach over the side—but he did, and he pulled the anchor up. We started moving. I kept us backing up while Josh pulled up the anchor. He finally got the anchor out of the water and hooked it on the gunwale. He looked pale and exhausted. I turned the skiff around and opened the throttle as far as it would go.

As we skipped across the rough water toward the welcoming dim lights of the marina, I said a prayer of thanks. I felt like Daniel, stretching his legs and blinking as he walked from the lions' den.

We didn't wake up until after 11:00 the next morning when Jessica knocked on the bedroom door. "You two better get up," she called from the other side of the door.

"We're tired," I yelled back to her. "We're going to sleep a little longer."

"But that big, weird guy in 213 told me you guys were having a lunch meeting," she told me. "It's nearly noon."

Apparently we were supposed to meet Mr. Vance at the Deep End Diner, and apparently he expected us to buy him lunch. There was nothing we could do—we got up, pulled on our jackets, and rode our bikes through the rain to the diner. At the door of the diner, Josh and I emptied our pockets. We only had about eleven dollars between us.

Inside, Mr. Vance was wedged into the same booth as last time, studying the menu. Several large grocery bags were lined up on the floor next to him. "Boys," he said when he saw us coming. "It's good to see you. I think I've got our ending all worked out. But let's order first."

Mr. Vance told the waiter he wanted a lobster roll and a cup of coffee, so Josh and I just ordered two ice waters. We couldn't afford anything else.

When the waiter left, Mr. Vance leaned confidentially over the table. "I've worked it out," he said. "I've got everything we need to blow that monster sky high. And you won't believe the price I got." He nodded down at the grocery bags on the floor next to him. Josh and I scooted farther away from them.

"All we need now is some bait," Mr. Vance said. "That's where you two come in."

Bait? I pictured myself dangling over the bay, suspended by a rope from a helicopter. I glanced over at Josh. He looked as worried as I was. "We've got two sisters," Josh offered.

Mr. Vance considered it a moment and then shook his head. "We can't use real people," he told us. "The medical bills wreak havoc with a budget." He looked wistfully out the window at the rainy street. "I learned *that* the hard way."

"So what *are* we going to use as bait?" Josh asked.

"I'm going to need you two to make a dummy out of some old clothes," he said. "You take care of that, and I'll take care of the bomb." He looked at me. "Is this storm going to keep up?" he asked.

"It's not supposed to clear out until tomorrow morning," I said. "It'll be raining tonight, if that's what you want to know."

"Perfect," he said. "We'll do it tonight."

Josh and I spent the whole afternoon up in a corner of the attic making a dummy out of old clothes. We took our time—it was nice and warm up there because of the rising heat from the kitchen. And the rain, much lighter now, fell softly on the roof above our heads.

Mr. Vance told us to make the dummy look as real as possible and to leave the middle part empty so he could load it with explosives. We were supposed to meet him in his room at 8:00, when he'd explain the whole plan to us.

"What do you suppose he's going to put in here?" Josh asked me, as we sat on the floor with the dummy between us. "Do you really think he found some dynamite or something?"

"Where in *this* town would they sell dynamite?" I said.

Josh shrugged. "Maybe at the sporting goods store," he said. "I hear it's an effective way to fish."

I laughed. "Maybe we should tell Pete," I said. "He can use all the help he can get."

Just then, Bonnie's head poked up through the attic door. "All right," she said accusingly. "What's going on here? What are you two up to?"

Josh jumped. He glanced guiltily at me and then back at Bonnie. "Nothing," he said. "We're not doing anything." But it was obvious from the way he said it that we *were* up to something.

Bonnie climbed into the attic and came over to where we were working. She stood over us with her hands on her hips. "Jessica said you guys met that big weird guy for lunch," Bonnie said. "And now he's in the backyard pouring Pepsi in the bushes, and you're up here making some kind of dummy. Something is *definitely* going on."

"*Nothing* is going on," I told her. I glared at Josh, hoping to keep him quiet.

"He's pouring Pepsi in the bushes?" Josh asked.

"Yeah," she said. "He's got a bunch of two liter bottles, and he's emptying them in the backyard. What are *you* guys doing?"

"None of your business," I told her. "What are you doing here anyway?"

"Mom dropped me off," she said. "I'm spending the night in Jessica's room."

Great! Just what I needed! "Well, stop snooping," I told her.

"I'm not snooping," she said. "Josh's mom sent me up here to tell you guys to wash up for dinner."

At the word *dinner,* my stomach rumbled. I hadn't had anything to eat all day.

"Great," Josh said. "I'm starving. What's for dinner?"

"Well, since I'm here, your mom's making a big broccoli casserole," Bonnie said. "Very thoughtful of her, huh?"

After dinner, Josh and I sneaked upstairs to room 213. We stood outside the door a moment.

"You sure you want to go through with this?" I asked Josh.

"Not really," he said. "But what choice do we have?"

He was right. If we didn't go out tonight and rid the bay of the monster, innocent lives would be in danger. And if Mr. Vance had a plan, the least we should do was hear him out.

I was just about to knock on Mr. Vance's door when the door to the room across the hall opened suddenly.

"I *knew* it!" Bonnie said, standing in the doorway of the empty room. "Didn't I tell you they'd come up here?"

Jessica appeared in the doorway next to her. "You were right," she said.

"Spill it, guys," Bonnie said, her hands on her hips. "If you don't tell us what you're up to, I'm going to tell."

"We're not up to anything," I told her, but I knew she didn't believe me.

"It has something to do with the big weird guy in there," she said, pointing to room 213. "And whatever it is, Jessica and I want in on it."

I thought about how Josh had volunteered them for monster bait and smiled. "I'm not sure you really want to be involved," I told her. "Much as I'd like to, I—"

At that instant, Mr. Vance's door ripped open, and he stood in the doorway looking down at us. Jessica gave a little squeal.

"Brilliant!" he said. "You've brought some new recruits. We can use the help." He stuck his head out in the hallway and looked both ways. "Come on in," he said. "The coast is clear." He stood back from the doorway so we all could enter.

As she stepped through the door, Bonnie gave me her most irritating smile.

Chapter 7

S o, you say there's a monster in the bay," Bonnie said skeptically. She held up the emptied Pepsi bottle, which was now crammed full of Alka Seltzer tablets. "And you're going to kill it with this?"

We were all crowded around the desk in Mr. Vance's room, where he was explaining his plan to us—sketching it out with a felt pen on a pad of yellow paper. Bonnie was having a great time. She didn't believe a word we'd told her.

"Monster attacks dummy," Mr. Vance explained with enthusiasm. "Bottles inside dummy break. Water gets in. Pressure builds. Monster explodes."

"So the monster's going to *explode?*" Bonnie said doubtfully.

"They always do," Mr. Vance assured her.

Bonnie kept a straight face. "Well, I want to be part of this plan," she said. "I wouldn't miss it for the world." I knew she just wanted to come along so she could make fun of me every step of the way—and no doubt to use it as ammo for years to come.

Mr. Vance looked over at me. "She's a bright one," he told me in a loud whisper. "She picked it up like *that*." He snapped his fingers. "It was a good idea to bring her along."

I just nodded. I didn't want any credit for inviting Bonnie along.

I stared down at the pad of paper on the desk. This was the plan: Josh and Mr. Vance would use my key to sneak up in the lighthouse tower when everyone was asleep. From there they would inform us of the monster's movements by walkie-talkie. Jessica, Bonnie, and I would take the skiff out on the bay. I'd get close to the monster, and Bonnie and Jessica would drop the "monster bomb" overboard. Then we'd race out of the way before the big explosion.

"OK," Mr. Vance said. "We're all set." He held out one of the two walkie-talkies he'd bought at the drugstore. "I'll call you on this when it's time to rendezvous."

Josh took the walkie-talkie. He held it in his

hand and looked down at it like he'd never seen one before. He looked at Mr. Vance. "No offense," he said. "But shouldn't we have some kind of adult supervision?"

In the darkness of Josh's garage, we put the dummy into one of the empty plastic trash cans lined up against the side wall. We needed to keep it dry, and this seemed like the best way. We sealed the lid tight.

Mr. Vance backed his Cadillac up to the open garage door and popped the trunk.

"You and Jessica load the trash can into the trunk," I told Bonnie. "If you're going to come along, you might as well be useful."

I took Josh aside. "You ready?" I asked him.

"I guess," he said. "I'm just glad I don't have to go out in the boat."

"I'd rather be in the boat than up in the tower," I told him.

"Even under these circumstances?" Josh asked.

"You mean with the monster out there in the bay?"

"No," he said. "I mean with *those two* in the boat with you."

I laughed. Bonnie and Jessica struggled to lift the big plastic trash can into the open trunk. "Just

give me the signal, and I'll push them overboard,"
I told Josh. Mr. Vance sat in the driver's seat of his
Cadillac, listening to the radio and playing his
steering wheel like a conga drum. "Are *you* going
to be OK with *him?*" I asked.

Josh grinned at me. "Just give me the signal,
and I'll push him off the tower," he said.

Mr. Vance backed his Cadillac up to the marina
entrance and popped the trunk open. Bonnie,
Jessica, and I piled out of the backseat into the
cold rain. Josh stayed up front with Mr. Vance.
"Good luck," Josh said. "I'll be praying."

"Thanks," I told him. "I was planning to do a
lot of that myself." I closed the car door.

Jessica and Bonnie went around to the back of
the car to get the trash can out of the trunk.

"Make sure the lid doesn't come off," I said.
"We don't want that thing to get wet before it's
supposed to."

"You *could* help," Bonnie said. "This thing is
pretty heavy."

"I'm the pilot," I told her. "You two are the
bombardiers."

I went around to the driver's side, and Mr.
Vance rolled the window down a crack.

"Remember," he said. "Stay put until Josh and I

are in position. We'll give you the signal." He held up his walkie-talkie. "Got yours?"

I patted the pocket of my jacket. "Right here," I told him. "I'll switch it on as soon as I'm in the skiff." Mr. Vance rolled the window up again.

"Come on, Danny," Bonnie said. "You can help carry this." She slammed the trunk.

"You heard the director," I told her. "I'm in charge of the boat; you two are in charge of the monster bomb."

They dragged the trash can out from behind the Cadillac, and Mr. Vance started up the engine. The lights came on, and the car pulled away, its red taillights illuminating the falling rain.

Bonnie, Jessica, and I sat in the skiff, huddled together next to the dock, while the rain began to come down harder. I'd pulled my plastic tarp from the skiff's locker and we held it over our heads to stay dry. We must have waited there for nearly an hour before the walkie-talkie crackled to life.

I must have dozed off, because it took me a few seconds to realize what the sound was. I pulled the walkie-talkie out of my jacket.

"Hello?" I said. "Skiff to lighthouse. Hello?"

"We're in position," Josh told me. "We've got you in sight."

I looked across the bay at the revolving beacon of the lighthouse. Sure enough, there were two dark specks up there in front of the light. "I can see you too," I said into the walkie-talkie.

Why did I have to be afraid of heights? Why couldn't I be the one up in the lighthouse tower with the other walkie-talkie, instead of the one trying to pilot a small skiff up next to a huge sea monster?

I grabbed the cold, wet cord on the engine and gave it a yank. The engine started up on the first try. I untied us, and we chugged out into the choppy deep waters of the bay.

It was a miserable night for boating. My shoes were soaked through and my ears ached from the cold wind coming in off the ocean. I pulled my jacket tighter around me and squinted into the rain. My face was numb. Jessica and Bonnie were huddled up near the front of the skiff wrapped in my blue plastic tarp. The big trash can was propped in the bow, its lid still sealed tight. When we got the signal from the lighthouse tower, the girls would pry off the lid and dump the dummy overboard. Everything was ready.

When we were in the middle of the bay, I raised the walkie-talkie to my lips. "Any sign of the monster?" I asked.

"Not yet," Josh's voice crackled on the walkie-talkie. "Maybe it's not raining hard enough."

"From where I sit, it's raining pretty hard," I told him.

"Well maybe we should—" Josh stopped talking in midsentence.

"Hello?" I said into the walkie-talkie. "Hello? I'm no longer receiving your transmission." There were a few seconds of static. I shook the walkie-talkie. Had the rain short-circuited it?

"He's here," Josh's voice said excitedly. "He's right in front of you. Maybe fifty yards."

I put the engine in neutral and coasted through the dark choppy water. I cautiously stood and peered out over the waves. "I can't see a thing," I told Josh.

"Trust me," Josh said. "It's right there, and it's huge."

"Get a little closer, son," Mr. Vance's voice boomed through the walkie-talkie. "He's got to see the bait."

I sat down and took the till again. We chugged slowly ahead, cautiously scanning the water for any sign of the monster.

"Better open the trash can," I called up to Bonnie and Jessica. "Time to get out the monster bomb."

Bonnie grinned back at me. "Sure thing, Captain," she said. It was clear she still didn't believe there was any monster, but Jessica's face seemed a little pale.

"We're getting out the bomb," I said into the walkie-talkie. "Are we still on course?"

"It's dead ahead and closing," Josh's voice told me.

Bonnie and Jessica kneeled on either side of the trash can and pulled the lid off. For a few seconds, both of them stared down into the trash can.

"Come on, you two," I called up to them. "Get a move on."

In unison, they both turned their faces blankly to me.

"What's the matter?" I asked them.

Jessica reached into the trash can and pulled out a backpack. "I've been looking for this for months," she said.

"What?" I yelled. "How did *that* get in there? Where's the bomb?"

Bonnie peered down into the trash can. She looked back at me and shook her head. "It's not in there."

It was one of those moments when everything seems to come rushing in on you. Here I was, out in the middle of a rainstorm in a little skiff, with a giant monster closing in on me—and the one weapon I had to defend myself with was gone.

I pointed at Jessica. "This is *your* fault!" I yelled at her. "I shouldn't have let you anywhere near the bomb. It's probably in *Venezuela* by now!"

"It's not *her* fault," Bonnie said, sticking up for her friend. "You were there when we loaded it up. We must have grabbed the wrong trash can. Besides, what does it matter? It's not a *real* bomb. And there's not *really* a monster out there."

"Do you have any idea the danger we're in?" I sputtered. *"In about a minute we're—"*

The crackle of the walkie-talkie cut me off. *"Now!"* Josh's voice came over the air. *"Drop the bomb now! It's coming right at you!"*

I stood and looked at the storm-tossed ocean in front of us. Sure enough, a massive dark shape slipped silently through the water toward us. In a panic I fumbled with the engine, trying to reverse it—but it stalled.

"Help!" I yelled into the walkie-talkie. *"Mayday!* We lost the bomb. We're stalled. What do I do *now?"*

Mr. Vance's voice boomed out of the walkie-talkie. I held it away from my face. "Don't worry, son," he said. "This is just what we need. It's a terrific plot twist. There's going to be some other way to kill the monster, and you'll find it at the last minute. It *always* happens that way."

"What?" I yelled into the walkie-talkie. I couldn't believe what I was hearing. "This isn't one of your stupid movies. I don't have any other way to kill the monster."

"The flare gun in the locker," Josh's voice crackled over the walkie-talkie. "Use the flare gun."

It was brilliant. "Good idea," I said into the walkie-talkie. "Bonnie!" I yelled. "Open the locker up there. Get out the flare gun."

Bonnie scrambled up to the front of the skiff and opened the locker door. She was still smiling, enjoying the game.

"Are you sure that will make it explode?" Mr. Vance's voice asked. "The monster's got to explode."

Here I was, about to be eaten—and all *he* cared about was getting a good explosion. I held the walkie-talkie to my lips. "Push him, Josh," I said into it. "Push him now."

"I've got it!" Bonnie yelled from the front of the boat. She held the flare gun in the air, still grinning.

"OK," I said. "Now shoot it at the monster."

Bonnie stood in the front of the boat, her feet spread apart, and aimed the flare gun down at the water. A huge shadow moved through the water toward us. A finger of light from the lighthouse swept across the water in front of us. A long tangle of writhing tentacles shimmered just below the surface.

Bonnie looked over her shoulder at me. Her face was suddenly pale, and her mouth hung open. She'd seen the monster. It had finally dawned on her that we were telling the truth. She turned back to face the monster and just stood there in the bow, the flare gun pointing down at the water, frozen in shock.

"Hurry!" I shouted. *"Pull the trigger!"*

Bonnie stood there, frozen. The shadow crept under the boat. She looked back at me utterly bewildered.

"Shoot it!" I yelled. *"Shoot it now!"*

Bonnie looked at the massive shadow in the water and then back at me, even more confused. Her lips moved a few seconds before sound came out. "I can't," she croaked. "I'm a vegetarian."

"What?" I couldn't believe my ears. If only the monster was a vegetarian, we wouldn't be in this mess!

"Come back here and take the till," I ordered.

Bonnie, as if sleepwalking, made her way back to where I was sitting. I grabbed the flare gun from her, and she took my seat at the till. "Keep it pointed at the lighthouse," I told her and clambered up to the bow of the skiff. I looked down at the water. The shadow was all around us now.

I took a deep breath and stood on wobbly legs. The skiff pitched and swayed under my feet. "Hold her steady," I yelled back at Bonnie. I knew she'd never piloted a boat before. I held the flare gun with both hands and pointed it down at the massive shadow on the water.

The light from the lighthouse swung around over the water. It lit up the huge rubbery mass of the monster's body. A long gray tentacle rose out of the water and reached, dripping, for the boat. I tried to hold my shaking hands steady as I squeezed the trigger.

At that exact moment, a big swell passed under the skiff, and I was pitched backward. As I fell— as if in slow motion—I saw the red flare rocket uselessly into the sky. I flung out my arms to break my fall and my hand glanced off the metal anchor hooked on the gunwale.

As I lay on my back in the middle of the skiff, I heard a splash and the rattling sound of the chain running over the side of the skiff. I'd knocked the anchor overboard.

The chain zipped over the side of the skiff and tore down through the water. There was no way to stop it. It would rip up my hands if I tried to grab it. I pulled myself to my feet and looked around at the water. The long tentacles writhed in the water to port and starboard. The monster was directly under us.

Bonnie screamed. Jessica was curled up in the back of the boat like it was an earthquake drill. I thought I could hear her praying. I stood there numb and helpless, looking around inside the skiff for some kind of weapon. There was nothing I could do.

I lifted the walkie-talkie to my mouth. I pressed the button and tried to think of some last words. But before I could, the skiff lurched suddenly forward. I fell back again, sprawled in the middle of the skiff. I heard the walkie-talkie plop into the water.

"What's happening?" Bonnie said, her voice full of panic. "We're moving."

She was right. The skiff was slowly moving through the water. I scrambled to the stern. The engine was still off, but we were definitely picking up speed. I looked back. The skiff wasn't just drifting—we were leaving a wake behind us. We were being towed through the water.

"Oh, no!" I said. "I think I hooked it with the anchor." The skiff lurched beneath me again. We were being towed toward the mouth of the bay and the open ocean. "It's pulling us out to sea. What do we do now? We've hooked the sea monster!"

"I told you fishing was barbaric," was all Bonnie could think of to say.

I started up the engine again and put it in reverse. We slowed a bit, but we were still being dragged toward the mouth of the bay. I revved the engine, still in reverse, but we didn't go backward. We just fishtailed from side to side as we picked up more and more forward speed. It was useless. I shut the engine off.

I looked up at the lighthouse and waved my arms frantically. Without the walkie-talkie, there was no way to tell them what was going on. Did they realize that the monster was towing us out to sea so he could eat us?

We passed beyond the breakwater, and suddenly the huge swells of the open sea raised and dropped us dizzingly. We were in deep, unprotected water now, and we immediately picked up speed.

No one could help us now. I bowed my head in silent prayer. "Lord," I prayed. "I'm in a really tough situation, and I need Your help. I know You're always there for us. I know You sealed the lions' mouths and delivered Daniel. Please do the same for us. Help us escape from the monster. I'll never ever ask for anything ever again if You save me now. Please, Lord."

I opened my eyes to find myself still in a storm, still on a skiff being pulled out to the open sea. I looked back toward the land. The lighthouse beacon was already fading into the rainy distance.

How long before a long rubbery tentacle snaked itself over the gunwale and wrapped itself around me like a boa constrictor? I imagined being pulled down through the cold salty water. I felt woozy.

But instead of just feeling bad for myself, I felt bad for Bonnie and Jessica. They had had no idea what they were getting into when they stepped into Mr. Vance's room tonight to hear the plan. They had had no idea they were stepping into a lion's den. Until a few minutes ago—when she finally saw the monster—this had just been a game to Bonnie. But now she was in the same boat as I. It was all my fault.

Jessica sat near the middle of the skiff facing me. She held tight to the gunwale and her lips moved in silent prayer. I looked at Bonnie huddled in the rain next to me. She was pale and shaking. I put my arm around her.

I'd never admit it, but at that moment I realized that, despite all her annoying habits, I loved my sister. She was a pain in the neck, and she drove me crazy most of the time, but she was a good kid, and I was blessed to be her brother. I sighed. Why had I waited until the end to realize that simple truth?

"What's that?" Jessica asked suddenly. She was looking behind us.

I glanced over my shoulder and saw the unmistakable lights and outline of a big fishing boat coming out of the bay. I waved my arms frantically. It was our only hope. But what were the chances that a passing fishing boat would see a little skiff on a big ocean in the middle of a storm?

"Do you think it can see us?" Jessica asked hopefully. She waved her arms above her head. "Do you think it knows we're here?"

As if in answer to our question, a huge spotlight came on aboard the fishing boat, and a disk of bright light zigzagged across the stormy water until the blinding beam fell upon us. I covered my eyes with one arm and continued to wave with the other.

In a few minutes the boat fell in beside us. It was Pete. "Are you in trouble?" Pete's voice rang out over the boat's loudspeaker. "We saw a flare go up."

I cupped my hands around my mouth. "It's me," I shouted. "We're hooked to a sea monster, and we have nothing to cut us loose."

Pete appeared on deck and hung over the rail shouting to us. "You hooked a what?"

"A sea monster," I shouted.

"It's true," Bonnie said. "We've all seen it."

I just wanted Pete to give me something to cut the anchor chain, but he insisted on splicing our anchor line onto his fishing boat's winch. He hadn't caught anything in weeks, and the idea of reeling in a monster appealed to him.

The three of us sat in the cabin of his fishing boat wrapped in warm blankets while the winch struggled to pull in the monster. We tried to explain to Pete what had happened, but we were all talking at once, and he had no idea who to listen to.

The cabin door burst open, and Jeff, the shipmate, stood in the doorway. "You'd better come look at this," he said. "You're not going to believe what we've got."

The four of us scrambled out onto the rainy deck and followed Jeff to the prow of the boat. I looked over the rail. Giant tentacles churned the water, and a rubbery body bobbed on the surface.

"See," I said. "I told you it was a sea monster."

Pete laughed. "That's no monster," he said. "That's a giant squid. I've only seen one once before. What was it doing in so close to land?"

"It must have been driven in here by the storms," Jeff said. "I'll bet this guy's why the fishing's been so bad in these parts."

Pete wanted to tow the squid in to shore, but Bonnie the Vegetarian insisted that we take it further out to sea and cut it free. Pete radioed ashore to tell our parents that we were safe, and by the first light of dawn, we were safely docked back in the marina. Officer Borders was there with the police cruiser to take us home.

I couldn't sleep when I got home. I went up to my room awhile and prayed. I thought about the important lessons I'd learned: about trusting God, about not jumping to conclusions, and about being kind to your annoying little sister.

When I smelled bacon frying, I went down to the kitchen for breakfast.

Chapter 8

W ell, it's not exactly the ending I'd hoped for, but there was plenty of suspense," Mr. Vance said. "It was a good story. All it really needed was an explosion." Josh and I were sitting in the booth at the Deep End Diner with him. Empty plates and glasses littered the table. Mr. Vance had actually volunteered to pay for lunch this time.

"A good story?" Josh said. "The people in this town are going to laugh at us for decades."

"It's not like we don't deserve it," I pointed out.

By breakfast time we'd worked it all out. Officer Borders had explained to us that the fancy sailboat we'd rescued had simply broken loose from its moorings at the marina and drifted out into the bay in the storm. And Jeffrey's family was back from their visit to their aunt down in San Francisco. Jessica had to give back the fishing rods she'd found. The owners had gone to buy some bait and reported them stolen when they came back to the dock and found their rods missing.

To make a long story short: there was an explanation for everything that happened. To make it even shorter: Josh and I were idiots.

The waiter brought us our check, and Mr. Vance handed him a credit card. "I'm going to need a receipt," Mr. Vance said. "This is a working lunch." The waiter nodded and withdrew.

"A working lunch?" I said.

"Sure," Mr. Vance said. "This is the first meeting for my next project: *Return to Terror Cove.*"

I looked at Josh. *"Return to Terror Cove?"*

"Possibly my best feature yet," Mr. Vance said. "A comedy horror movie. Two young lads and their plucky sisters go after the sea monster in their boat."

"Their skiff," I corrected him.

"And using their ingenuity, the young heroes blow the monster sky high."

"We didn't blow anything up," Josh pointed out. "Why does everything have to end with an explosion? Couldn't it be a little more realistic?"

"Well, how *else* are we going to end it?" Mr. Vance said.

I looked over at Josh. He shrugged.

"I don't know," I said. "How about the two boys learn some kind of important lesson?"

Josh nodded. "Yeah," he said. "And it can end up like *this,* with the characters sitting around in a coffee shop talking."

Mr. Vance looked at us a few seconds and then threw his head back and bellowed with laughter. He slapped the tabletop with his hand while he tried to catch his breath. "I'm sorry," he said, his eyes watering. "It'll never work. I know endings. And a coffee shop is a pretty stupid place to end a story."

"He's got a point there," Josh said.

Don't miss another exciting

Heebie Jeebies

adventure!

Turn the page to check out a chapter from

Piranha Picnic

Chapter 1

We couldn't have picked a worse day for a picnic.

The grass felt like a green sponge from all the rain. My dad had to spread a blue tarp beneath the quilt to keep us from getting soaked. He wanted my mom to be comfortable on our last day together. She had an opportunity she couldn't pass up. Tomorrow she'd be gone.

We were at the riverpark not far from our house. A dreary sky kept us company, along with a blue heron wading near the bank. After missing a fish, the bird let out a deep croak and flapped its giant wings.

So much for the heron.

We were supposed to be enjoying some family time before my mom left us. Normally, we weren't what you would call a real talkative family.

Today we were mute.

I sat cross-legged on the patchwork quilt. A giant beef rib waited for my teeth. The paper plate soaked up the red juice. So did the chips, now soggy. I wasn't hungry, which for me was unheard of. I'm thirteen, have a wiry build, and weigh 140 pounds. But don't bc misled; I eat like a horse.

"I still can't believe the river," my dad observed. "I've never seen it this high."

My older sister, Sandy, looked up from her novel. "It's scary." A pink ribbon secured her brown hair in a ponytail. She was sixteen and always reading. Teachers loved her.

I tossed a twig into the chocolate current and watched it drift south. "No, it's not."

The Red River bordered the north side of our town, not in a straight line, but an *S* pattern. Normally it meandered along kind of slow and peaceful. But with all the rain, it had picked up speed . . . and space. Until now, I'd never seen the river as a threat. The southern sun warmed the shallow water for a good seven months a year, making it the perfect place to swim or fish or drift on a raft.

Until now.

"You're sure quiet," my mom said to me.

I grabbed my fishing pole and stood up. "What's

to say?" I didn't want to be mean, I just didn't have anything to talk about.

"Nick, don't be that way," my mom called after me.

I waded knee-deep into the river. The water smelled like strong tea and felt almost as warm. A giant willow tree—usually on dry ground—split the current. A thick limb that reached over the water had my name on it. I climbed up and straddled the limb. My lure resembled a silver minnow. I gave it a cast and reeled it in, hoping for a lunker. The disciples had gone fishing when Jesus left them. My parents couldn't blame me for this.

"Nick, you should eat," my mom said.

"Let him starve!" my sister yelled in my direction.

Mom walked to the water's edge carrying the paper plate with the beef rib and chips. I pretended not to notice her.

"Nick, come and get this," she said. She stood on the bank, afraid to venture into the water. The horror of nearly drowning as a little girl still haunted her. She held out the plate.

I stayed put and focused on my next cast. I landed the silver lure fifty feet out, let it drift, then reeled in. The sound of movement against the current caught my attention. I turned to see my mom sloshing through the water. It rose to her shins, then her knees. She kept coming and put the plate on the limb in front of me.

"This was long overdue," she said.

I forced myself to be happy for her. "Way to go, Mom. But I'm still not hungry."

"Nick, you're always hungry." She nudged my side. "Come on. Eat."

I continued to reel the lure through the leaf-stained water. "In a minute. A few more casts."

My mom asked me if I wanted to talk. I shook my head and wouldn't look at her until she sloshed away.

My dad greeted her on the bank with a hug and encouraging words.

My sister joined them. "I'm proud of you, Mom."

They lingered for a moment, then returned to the quilt.

I was still watching them when the fish struck. I couldn't believe it. The minnow lure was so close I had practically lifted it from the water to cast again. I yanked the pole to set the hook. The line sliced across the current. The fish had to be a lunker. It bolted upstream, then circled back. The fight was on. I pictured a ten-pound bass with fierce eyes and a powerful tail. A trophy! Maybe things weren't so bad after all.

Without a net, there was only one way to land it—wade to the bank and drag the giant ashore. I balanced carefully and brought one leg over the limb.

Plunk!

Bummer. I knocked the plate into the water. The rib sank. The plate and chips floated downstream. Oh, well. This was a once-in-a-lifetime fish. I glanced at the water, ready to slide from the limb. I yanked on the pole and gave the reel a few turns. Too easy. The tension was gone.

"No," I moaned. I turned the handle. No resistance. The line went slack. The lunker had thrown the hook. I reeled in, praying the tension would return. It didn't.

No trophy. No fish. I lifted the lure from the water, determined to cast again. Then I saw the damage. Whatever I had hooked had chomped the lure in two.

A swirling beneath me caught my attention. I peered into the water. A fin broke the surface. Then another. A tail splashed. Greenish-brown. The water churned, boiled. Tails. Fins.

Then it stopped. The water flowed like before. No fish. Just ripples. I bent forward and searched the water. I saw something. Long, smooth. What was it? I remembered the rib. But it was covered with sauce and meat when it fell in. I got on my stomach and hugged the limb. I lowered my face to the surface. It sure looked like the rib bone.

But no bass or bluegill could have devoured it that quickly. A catfish would have picked the whole thing up and swam off. I went down the list of fish. Carp. Gar. Suckers. None of those could have cleaned the bone that fast.

I stared into the water. Maybe it wasn't the rib after all. Maybe it was just a smooth stick. Or a pipe. I started to reach for it, but couldn't. I used my fishing pole instead. I pushed the tip under the white whatever-it-was and lifted. It came to the surface, then started to fall. I grabbed it just in time. The rib. Clean. White. Not a shred of meat on it.

Something sharp had scraped it clean.

I thought of the minnow lure with its steel shank snapped in two. A meaty rib scraped to the bone. I stared at the dark water, the water I would have to wade through in bare feet to get to shore. My mom leaving us made me sad. But this was different.

This was scary.